WALKING WEST ON THE CAMINO

Encore Une Fois
(One More Time)

**Walking West on the Camino—
Encore Une Fois**

Copyright © 2017
by Johnna Studebaker

www.johnnastudebaker.com
www.walkingwestonthecamino.com
www.twopelerinespress.com

All rights reserved. No part of this book may be reproduced or transmitted in any form or by any means, electronic or mechanical, including photo-copying, recording, or by any information storage and retrieval system without the written permission of the publisher, except where permitted by law.

Text and Oil Paintings:
Johnna Studebaker

Book Design:
Kenesson Design, Inc.

ISBN: 978-0-9992424-0-7
LCCN: 2017949965

Two
Pèlerines
Press

Santa Fe, NM

WALKING WEST ON THE CAMINO

Acknowledgments

I am deeply grateful to the following: Charlie Kenesson, my book designer extraordinare. Suzan Hall, my very helpful content editor. My good friends, Barbara Taylor and Catherine Sherman, who read my book in its early stages and wholeheartedly cheered me on. Marcia Pyner, my twin sister, who has made me a better person all my life. Angel, my dear little Siamese cat, who insisted that she sit in my lap while I wrote this book, but then died just before its publication. The Holy Spirit, my muse, who showed up just in the nick of time to bring form to my jumbled thoughts.

Table of Contents

Introduction 1
I. Le Puy-en-Velay to Figeac—Spring 2011 9
   Saint James at the Le Puy Cathedral of Notre Dame ...20
   Black Madonnas at the Le Puy Cathedral 21
   Chapel of Saint Michel d'Aiguilhe
   with Guido Reni's Michael 24
   The Église de Saint-Pierre-de-Bessuéjouls 42
   Rue du College in Estaing 45
   "Mystical Rose" at Abbaye Saint-Foy in Conques 51
   Chapelle Saint-Roch, near the village of Noailhac 53
II. Figeac to Condom—Spring 2012 61
   Prayers laid at the foot of the cross outside Figeac 65
   Painted from Peter Paul Rubens' the
   Immaculate Conception 68
   The Pont Valentre over the Lot River leaving Cahors ..71
   Chapel Glow 75
   On the Camino au Printemps 79
   Iron cross on bridge near Auvillar 84
   Joan of Arc 86

III. Condom to Saint-Jean-Pied-de-Port—Spring 2013 ...95
The Château de Maintenon 99
Resting spot at the church at Lanne-Soubiran 106
The Église Notre Dame and the Porte d'Espagne
in Saint-Jean-Pied-de-Port 119

IV. Saint-Jean-Pied-de-Port to Burgos—Summer 2014 ..129
Alto del Perdón 136
Leafy Tunnel of Time 150

V. Burgos to León—Spring 2015 161
Wheat fields on the Meseta as far as the eye can see ...164

VI. León to Santiago de Compostela—Spring 2016 185
Our Lady of Guadalupe 189
1998—Swinging the Botafumeiro at the
Santiago Cathedral 202

Epilogue 217

Introduction

It was early one morning in June of 1998. I lay in bed trying to "figure it out," a phrase my twin sister said I use a lot, looking for meaning or a lesson behind things. Just how could this be? I peered over the covers to assess the situation. My left leg was propped up on a pillow, bluish in places, aching and sore. My swollen toes were sticking out of an ace bandage that wound up my leg like a snake. *Dear God, I don't understand. I don't get it.* I cried and then cried some more. Self pity and confusion were now my closest friends. I reached desperately for the Gideon Bible in the drawer by the bed and flipped to the Book of James. After all, shouldn't I find answers from the Great Apostle himself, who has inspired so many pilgrims through the ages, under the field of stars, on the great Camino to Santiago de Compostela?

We had such a fine flight over, my husband and I and one of our friends. They had planned this trip for months. As for me, I was along for the ride, or so I thought. I knew nothing about the Camino except for what I had read on the flight. We had flown from San Diego, where we lived at the time, to Madrid and then to Leon in northwestern Spain. I had purchased a special hand carved walking stick at the Samos Monastery near Leon, where we were starting our walk. It was beautiful and fragile and lovingly made. We had been prayed for and blessed by a little monk at the monastery. "*Buen Camino,*" he told us with a smile. As we walked down the long sidewalk leaving the monastery, I felt almost giddy with excitement and also grateful for the coming experience. Then it happened—a misstep, a slight twist of my foot as I stepped off the curb onto the paved road. I felt a disquieting pop within my very being, and I knew deep down in my soul that my Camino experience was about to take a turn I hadn't expected or bargained for. Of course, I tried to laugh it off, but as we walked on, the pain in my ankle began to grow, and persist, and then scream for my attention. I hobbled down the road until we could arrange for the nearest hotel room. I was devastated. *Why me, Dear God, and why now?* I would have done better to ask why *not* me, but more on that later.

And so, as I lay in bed sniveling, I read from the Book of James, hoping Saint James would help me bring meaning to this chaos, this twist of fate and ankle, and to my despair:

[T]he trying of your faith worketh patience. But let patience have her perfect work, that you may be perfect and entire, wanting nothing. James 1:2-4

Now just what did this have to do with me? I thought resentfully. Clearly patience wasn't my strongest virtue. I wondered what insight and comfort Saint James was trying to whisper to me. The message was obvious, of course, but I was feeling too sorry for myself to notice. I read on:

If any of you lack wisdom, let him ask of God,…and it shall be given him. But let him ask in faith, nothing waivering. For he that wavereth is like a wave of the sea driven with the wind and tossed. James 1:5-8

It clearly had to percolate. The words of a minister from my past resounded in my head. "Call it all good." I wondered what good could ever come out of this. My husband and our friend had set out early that morning to walk the Camino *without me.* They had rented a car and a driver to meet them at their stopping point for the day and then to transport them back to the hotel. By late afternoon, my husband returned to our room, full of cheery smiles and excitement, telling me about their splendid first day on the Camino. They had hiked along a lovely mountain ridge of laurel and other wild flowers. And, as he handed me a bouquet of purple posies, I decided then and there that they were not going to leave me behind again—not one more day of this. And so, I adjusted my attitude into a quiet but steely resolve to press on. Something must have slipped in by osmosis amid my tears. Clearly, Saint James was not done with me quite yet.

The next morning, bright and early, I sprang out of bed determined to carry on. And so we headed out, me on crutches. My husband had gotten some pain pills from his doctor before our trip in anticipation of the foibles we might encounter. An ironic joke, I might add, since his fears were realized by me. And so it was—my orientation and initiation into the Way of St. James, the Camino. God, that divine presence who seeks us as we seek Him, must have a sense of humor. We will see who gets the last laugh.

I had often pondered the idea of God. I was raised in a Protestant faith and had gone to Sunday school and church and even Bible school as a child. But, in my early adult years, I had pulled away to seek my own truth. I knew that this world wasn't necessarily as it seems, having experienced several strange and yet synchronistic events in my young life. For example, one lovely Saturday afternoon Daddy ran into his good friend Fiesty's house for a nip of whisky. Only he left us twins (Marcia and me—age five at the time) in the car parked at the top of a very steep hill out in front of the house. I can remember our panic and helplessness as apparently the parking brakes gave way and the car began to roll down the hill. We didn't know what to do. We watched as the car careened past two cross streets, and just before it reached the bottom of the hill and the ongoing traffic, it abruptly made a right turn at the last cross street and slowly came to a stop on the right side of the road at the curb, just as pretty as you please. Do angels have to take driver's education classes? Or was it the unseen hand of the Divine? I knew then something was up on this beautiful little planet earth of ours—something we only catch glimpses of, if we are lucky and pay attention.

I remember my nocturnal flights of fancy as a young child. I would fly out the upstairs bathroom window to visit our elderly friend Ms. Austin, who lived a few blocks away—she who fondly read us poems such as "Little Orphan Annie" in the afternoons. Marcia remembers going too, so don't scoff. As I grew older, I packed away my abilities to travel out-of-body. After all, it would have been too hard, I reasoned, to explain it to the adults around me. It became our little secret. I also, sadly, eventually forgot how. Was I in vivid imagination mode? Was it lucid dreaming? I don't think so. There is much we do not understand and can only surmise in this giant matrix of existence we call the universe.

My first Camino trip only confirmed my belief in the unseen world and in the mysteries of life. Now, let me tell you of my further adventures on the Camino de Santiago de Compostela pilgrimage and beyond. I am the ecstatic wanderer, and at times, the holy fool—or perhaps just simply a fool. Let us proceed, then, but this time we shall tread lightly, hand in hand, with faith, as we step out ever so carefully plodding terra firma.

The road to Santiago de Compostela is an ancient pilgrimage route which is third in importance and popularity only after the routes to Jerusalem and to Rome. The relics of Saint James are said to be buried at Santiago. James, the brother of John, was believed to be the first martyred apostle, beheaded by Herod Agrippa. It is also believed that the Apostle James had returned to Jerusalem after spending time on the Iberian Peninsula evangelizing. Legend has it that after he was stoned to death, his body was secreted away by his disciples by stone boat from the Holy City. The boat eventually landed in Pedron on the Galician coast of northwestern Spain. About 812, a hermit named Pelayo, led by a celestial vision, found what was thought to be St. James' grave in an old Roman cemetery in Galicia. The grave was discovered under a mantle of stars along the path of the Milky Way. And so sprang up the great Cathedral at Santiago de Compostela ("campus stellae" meaning in Latin "field of the star") that now houses the reputed remains or relics of Saint James—the one, who like his brother John, dropped his nets, and with most likely unaccustomed but great faith, left all to follow the great Master Jesus.

In medieval times, saints and sinners made the trek from all across Europe—for penance, for a miraculous cure, for wisdom and spiritual awakening, for adventure. Prisoners were sentenced to the Camino. Paupers and princes came. The Roman Catholic Church and the monks from Cluny in France were quick to sanction the site of Saint James and extracted favors and dispensations for the remittance of sins for the completion of the Way of St. James. They also most likely lined their own coffers. The Knights Templars, who were fresh from their exploits in Jerusalem, guarded the Camino. Pilgrim hospitals and hostels sprang up to house weary travelers and to minister to the sick and injured and dying. The pilgrimage to Santiago de Compostela also aided the cause of the re-conquest of Spain from the Moors during the Spanish Crusades. Saint James became the "Moor slayer" (*Santiago Matamoros* in Spanish) and was depicted riding his great steed with his sword hoisted high in battle. He was also portrayed as the pilgrim (*Santiago Peregrino* in Spanish; *Saint-Jacques Pèlerin* in French) treading the path with his scallop shell and his staff as he called the faithful to repentance and prayer.

Now, as then, the religious and the spiritual and the non-believers alike come—by bicycle, on horseback, on foot. Why, and in search of what? The answers are intensely personal and varied. It is said that the Camino lies along ley lines, part of a special energy grid that has attracted pilgrims since Celtic times, on a course directly under the Milky Way. This may explain some of it. The Camino calls its own in its unique and mysterious and powerful way, those with ears to hear. That day I stepped off the curb at the monastery in Samos, I clearly lacked wisdom and understanding—much less any comprehension of the Way of Saint James, spiritual or otherwise. But as it is so often said, "There are no accidents in life." There is evidence of this as my own Camino story unfolds.

There are a multitude of routes to Santiago de Compostela coming from Portugal, from southern Spain, and from the far reaches of Europe. From France, pilgrims follow several routes. They come from Vézelay south of Paris, from Tours and Bordeaux, and from Le Puy-en-Velay heading ever westward toward Santiago. About 951 A.D., Godescalc, the Bishop of Le Puy, who was fresh from his own pilgrimage to Santiago de Compostela, sanctioned the revival of the ancient Cathedral of Notre Dame at Le Puy as an early starting point for pilgrims on the Way. The Le Puy Route runs through France along the GR 65; it is almost five hundred miles long. It passes through the Auvergne region, Gascony, and Basque Country finally reaching Saint-Jean-Pied-de-Port on the French side of the Pyrenees. The *Camino Frances*, also called the French Route or the Jacobean Way, is perhaps the most popular and well known route. It begins at Saint-Jean Pied-de-Port (the gate for the armies of Charlemagne and later Napoleon) and also spans a distance of about five hundred miles. It winds through the Pyrenees to Roncesvalles (*Roncevaux* in French), on to Pamplona, and then through the Navarre, Castille-Leon, and Galician regions of northern Spain, eventually reaching Santiago de Compostela. The route continues ultimately to Finisterre on the Atlantic coast. In the Middle Ages, Finisterre was thought to be the end of the world.

On my initial Camino trek, we made it to Santiago de Compostela from Samos. I had hobbled on for roughly ninety-five miles. It was a sweet and precious time. I too had pressed my hand into the smooth deep recesses of the cool marble at the

Portico de Gloria at the entrance to the great Cathedral—fingerprints frozen in time. I had joined the ranks of those who had come before me. I wondered who they might be—those hopeful, desperate, longing, yet triumphant souls. Did they walk with St. James unawares? There is something about walking the Camino on crutches that humbles the soul and lays one bare. But then we all walk with crutches at times in our lives, in our darkest nights. Growing stronger in the journey, I had stared hopelessness and despair in the face and pressed on. I had also learned to be more patient and compassionate with myself and with others. I had learned not to push so much and to see that there is a divine timing or rhythm in all things.

I had my ankle x-rayed at a hospital in Santiago. There was nothing broken, just badly-torn ligaments. My husband and I walked part of the Le Puy Route the following year, from Le Puy to Conques, me without crutches that time. Conques is considered one of the most beautiful villages in France—it was sublime. I wish I could say that my husband and I lived happily ever after, but in 1999, our paths took a different turn. We divorced, parting as friends. I will always honor that time together and our experiences on the Camino. It was through him that my journey really began.

Fast forward to 2011: I have been a practicing attorney in Santa Fe for many years, representing children in child abuse and neglect cases as well as in juvenile delinquency defense. So, why am I drawn to the Camino after all these years? I have a busy and full life—perhaps too busy. Still, I long to walk the Camino again—so much so that I often wake up remembering the Camino having dreamed I was there once more. It haunts me and calls my name. Finally, twelve years after my first sojourn on the Camino de Santiago, I answer its plaintive call. And, I persuade my somewhat reluctant twin sister Marcia to come along. We are going *ensemble*—yes, together. I want so much for us to experience its beauty and mystery together. She indulges me, but only because she knows I will otherwise head out alone, like the fool in the Tarot who jumps off the precipice, her knapsack tied at the end of a pole flung across her shoulder. It has been said "Leap and the net will appear." This certainly applies to Saint James, to faith, and to those who walk the Way.

In the end, we backpacked almost one thousand miles in three-week segments each year over a period of six years, starting in Le Puy and ending at Santiago. The Camino called us back again and again. What started out for me as an incidental hiking adventure years ago, bloomed into a passionate journey of body and soul, so transfixed were we. Each year we added side trips to other places we wanted to visit, such as Paris, Chartres, Bordeaux, Madrid, and Avila. I have tried to capture some of their allure here as well.

As you will see soon enough, I have also rather cleverly prolonged my stay on the Camino by returning home and making paintings from some of my photographs. As I paint, I am suspended in timelessness, walking the Camino once more.

And so, let the quest begin. Or should I say, continue.

Buen Camino! Bon Chemin!

I.
Spring 2011
Le Puy-en-Velay to Figeac

158 MILES—14 DAYS

Le Puy-en-Velay, Montbonnet, Monistro-d'Allier,
Domaine du Sauvage, Saint-Alban-sur-Limagnole,
Aumont-Aubrac, Ferme des Gentianes, Aubrac,
Saint-Côme d'Olt, Estaing, Golinhac, Conques,
Livinhac, Figeac

Quicken me, O Lord, according to thy loving kindness. —Psalms 119: 159

Marcia doesn't really want to go. She distrusts my abilities to navigate our pilgrimage safely. But, here we are meeting up in the Atlanta Airport, both of us a little apprehensive, but wildly excited to see each other. The weight of my backpack is almost bowing me over, although I have already dumped my rolled sleeping pad into a trash can at the airport. Marcia looks no better off than I am. And seeing I have no pad, she politely pitches hers too. She must be wondering, *What has she gotten me into this time?* I reposition my backpack, and together we trudge down the terminal towards the international gates—both of us lugging our backpacks still.

I had just hosted a little gathering of neighbors on my patio the evening before. We took a "nay or yea" vote over wine as to what in that large stack of things before us was to go or stay: Mosquito net for head, nay; headlamp, nay; four pairs of socks, yea; small purse, yea; REI sleeping bag, yea; foam sleeping pad, yea (big mistake); clothesline, yea; camp cookware, yea; makeup and mascara, yea. You get the point.

As we approach the central waiting area, I notice a beautiful grand piano in the lobby. A pianist strides over, sits down, and begins to play John Lennon's "Let It Be" as if just for me. As the music wafts its way through the terminal, I think, *How odd*, and I smile to myself. It is my favorite song, and I had been playing it over and over before I left home. I, who have been so Type A, could do well to take the hint.

We decided to start in Le Puy-en-Velay in France and take the Le Puy Route. I had been brushing up on my high school and college French at the Travel Bug in Santa Fe. I was also cramming (as if I had an exam coming up) on the flight over. We have gotten little sleep. As we disembark the airplane, I nervously smile and ask a young French woman stationed in the middle of the terminal, *"Bonjour, Mademoiselle. Comment allez-vous? Parlez-vous anglais?"* I had been practicing for such a time as this. Yes, I am hoping that this woman is in a good mood and can speak English. I remember my conversational French class in college as if it were yesterday. It was a small class. None of us could speak French very well. We all kept our heads down, our eyes trained on the textbook, anxiously hoping we wouldn't get called on. Until one day, our clever French teacher brought in a blackboard pointer. She tapped me on the head first. *"Parlez-vous français! Parlez-vous français, Mademoiselle!"* Oh, that I could have been able to speak more French. Now, as I am standing in the middle of the Charles de Gaul Airport in Paris, I wish I had paid more attention.

Before we left, we were warned that you must ask the French how they are doing before proceeding to ask them anything else lest they consider you to be impolite. Smiling too much, I repeat, *"Comment allez-vous? Parlez-vous anglais?" Thank God she speaks English*, I think, as this nice French airport employee directs us in good English to a bus that will take us into central Paris. We have booked a hotel room at the Hilton near the Arc de Triomphe. It is gray and drizzling rain. We pull our plastic rain capes over our backpacks and duck our heads under awnings as we half-run several long blocks to the hotel. We are grateful to be here. There will be no Camino for us quite yet. Jet lagged and tired, we unpack and compare our supplies and repack and then sink into the comfort of the soft pillows and blankets. Sleep comes easily for us both.

As the next day dawns, we are already up. We savor our *petit déjeuner*—a small breakfast of warm buttery croissants with raspberry jam, steaming *café au lait*, and fresh-squeezed orange juice. We are then directed by the concierge to the nearest Metro station where we can take the Metro to Au Vieux Campeur. Our guidebook says we can purchase all sorts of hiking gear there. Hiking poles can no longer be carried on flights, so we are looking to find them in Paris. We get off at Place Maubert and locate several of these camping stores all in a city block tucked among the outdoor flower markets—REI French style. Mission accomplished, we stroll the Avenue des Champs-Élysées and end up at the Cathedral of Notre-Dame near the River Seine. Notre-Dame, with its flying buttresses, is a magnificent example of French Gothic architecture. *Quelle belle église*—a beautiful church indeed! We wait in line for almost an hour. It is worth it. This is not the first visit for me, but it is so for Marcia. The rose windows have beckoned us in. I have read that for some, just a glimpse of these exquisitely crafted stained glass windows brings states of ecstasy. In the Middle Ages, before the masses could read, these pictorial stories of Christianity offered hope and faith and beauty apart from the mundane. It is easy to see why. They glow hues of red and green and blue and gold in the sunlight.

Today, there is an exhibit within the Cathedral honoring Saint Teresa of Avila, the first female Doctor of the Catholic Church and a mystic. I was familiar with the mystical traditions, having studied St. Teresa and St. John of the Cross, her male counterpart, for several years. I am reminded of her most famous book, *The Interior Castle*, and its admonition to turn within and find peace in meditation and recollection. I have walked to the Carmelite Monastery in Santa Fe for their evening vespers for many years, having been guided there initially by an internal whisper. We leave Notre-Dame finally, I rather reluctantly, and walk through the splendid Jardin des Tuileries before we catch the yellow L'Open Tour Bus for a tourist's view around the city.

We are also eventually heading for the Montmartre district, just north of Paris central. Montmartre is, of course, famous for the Moulin Rouge and for the outpouring of art during the Belle Époque, when the likes of Dali, Monet, Toulouse-Lautrec, van Gogh, and Picasso came here to paint. We weave in and out of the delightful shops and the tourist haunts, and we later treat ourselves to *hors d'oeuvre et le vin rouge* (red wine) at a quaint café close by. We are toasting our good fortune to be in such a sweet spot on the planet. À *votre santé!* (literally, to your health!) The sky is a bright crystal blue, and it is starting to get hot. The beautiful white-domed Basilica of the Sacred Heart (*Sacré-Coeur*) sits high on a hill in this area—we walk over on the narrow cobblestone street in the shade of the tall trees. This magnificent Basilica, overlooking Paris, offers a spectacular panoramic view of the city. Finally, we catch the Metro back to the Hilton. It was a day well spent. *Belle Paris*—beautiful, beautiful Paris!

At first light, we are again navigating the Metro to the Gare de Leon on the east side of Paris, where we take the speed train (*le Train Grand Vitesse—TGV*) to Leon, changing at Saint-Etienne, and then on to Le Puy. Le Puy-en-Velay is a UNESCO World Heritage Site. *C'est une ville magnifique!* We have read that it is a magnificent starting point on the Camino. Only this afternoon as we approach, the dark sky has opened up a deluge which is streaming down the windows of the train. Nonetheless, it is not enough to dampen our spirits or our sense of adventure. We are Nancy and Fancy Drew—no shrinking violets are we. We are fortunate little girls who grew up in the 1950's and early 60's reading Nancy Drew mysteries; we were bold and brave as we hurried behind our heroine, Nancy, up the spiral staircase.

An Asian man and woman sitting across from us on the train are amused and curious as they hear our hushed chatter and laughter. I had struggled to get the door to the loo open and to get back to my seat as the train pulled out of the station. I manage a "bonjour" with a smile. The man responds in perfect English, "Where are you from, ladies?" with a twinkle in his eye, as if he didn't know. It seems smiles are the universal language of this world. And with that, we strike up a conversation. Kim, who was born in Cambodia, is an American citizen now living in California near Los Angeles. His sister Annie, who speaks French and no English, lives in Le Puy. They are returning together from their father's funeral which took place a few days before in Paris. Pelts of heavy rain continue to beat down on the windows of the train. But, once in Le Puy, like clockwork, they whisk us off—all of us running and laughing in the downpour—to their parked car where they transport us to our prearranged *gîte d' étape* in the old section of the city. And thus, the Camino delivers up its first kindness and synchronicity. We are amazed, but perhaps not too surprised.

A word about *gîtes d' étape*, also called *auberges* (*refugios* or *albergues* in Spanish): They are simple accommodations or hostels on the Camino provided for hikers, bicyclists, and in some places, pilgrims on horseback. No tourists are allowed. We hear stories of those who might be dropped off from their vehicles down the road from the gîte as a ruse to be able to qualify to stay in the facility. Bad juju—I don't recommend it. For those truly on the Way of St. James, some monasteries and convents house pilgrims in gîtes—dormitory style rooms with warm showers, bunk beds, and meals—as they have done for centuries. There are also municipally run gîtes and those set up privately. Some operate by donation only; others charge a modest fee. And, for a bit extra, there are four course meals shared at the community table with people from all walks of life and from around the world. But, you must be out by eight o'clock in the morning, if not earlier, as preparations are already under way for the next round of pilgrims.

Back in 1998 and 1999, on my first excursions on the Camino, our friend had rented a car and paid a driver to meet us at our hotels each evening with our luggage. None of us—not me, not my husband, not he—wanted to lug our bags on the trail. This was rather fortuitous, as it turned out, since I ended up walking on crutches on that trek. Neither did we want to stay in the gîtes. Instead, we stayed in two or three-star hotels and only barely noticed the gîtes as we walked by them. *What sorts would stay there?* we all wondered smugly as we peered in. We didn't really understand. Little did I know my resounding retort years later would be "*Me!*"

Marcia and I want the *true pilgrim experience*, or at least I do—backpacks and all. With that being said, we have already cheated a bit and called ahead from the Hilton and reserved beds at a lovely privately run gîte d' étape on the west end of Le Puy at 29 Rue des Capucins and Rue St. Jacques. When I say "cheated," I mean we haven't just let fate, or I should say the Camino, pick out our beds for the night. This gîte is positioned on the Camino as you head out of town. "*Bonjour, Madame, Comment allez-vous? Est-ce que vous parlez anglais?*" I ask. By now, it rolls off my tongue. The woman behind the desk smiles slightly, and after I point at our reservations and make similar gyrations, we are shown to our dormitory room. All is well that ends well—for now.

We hear from others at the gîte that the Friends of St. Jacque, an ex-pilgrim group, hosts a welcome social every evening to answer pilgrims' questions and to stamp their credentials. We scramble to arrange our things and then head for the gathering which is in the old section of Le Puy near the cathedral. We want to make sure our documents are in order, and we want to meet others just starting out on the Camino.

A word about pilgrim credentials, aka pilgrim passports: I had already ordered our passports off the internet from the Confraternity of Saint James, a British association for pilgrims. Pilgrim passports are required to stay in the gîtes on the Camino and are stamped nightly at your place of refuge. We are anxious to get ours stamped. We have read in our walking guide that gîtes and even some churches will place their stamp in your book. It is official recognition that you are walking the Camino—blood, sweat, and tears. At the end of the pilgrimage, in Santiago de

Compostela, your reward is a beautifully prepared *Compostela*, or certificate, in Latin, marking the completion of your journey.

The reception is festive. We meet a French woman who has also been fussing with her backpack trying to decide what to take and what to discard. We are all painfully aware by now that if we choose to take those certain favorite but useless things, we will be carrying them on our backs like an albatross. This is a sobering thought indeed. We arrange to meet our new acquaintance later that evening in a lovely café for a bowl of lentils, hearty farm bread, and a glass of red wine. Lace curtains hang daintily from the windows all around. Le Puy, we have learned, is known for its lentil soup and its *dentelle*, or lace shops. Marcia is a little anxious. She is asking a lot of questions to try to allay her fears. Marcia is a strong and independent woman, an artist, a former art teacher, and for many years now, a flight attendant. She is an experienced traveler. She is also little comforted. The Camino hasn't called her yet, it seems. I am hoping it will. By now, the French woman is somewhat irritated by it all. I suspect she doesn't want to be reminded of her own anxieties. She wants to remain positive—rightly so. She explains she is leaving very early the next morning. We hope to see each other again. Alas, we never do.

The beautiful Romanesque Cathedral of Notre Dame, which is in the ancient part of town, hosts a pilgrim mass at seven every morning. We make a note to go, but this means checking out early. Back at our gîte, I drift into sleep thinking about the events of the day. I am glad to be here. I am glad to be alive this very moment. And, I am happy Marcia and I are on this quest together. I do love Marcia so.

We have checked out early and are winding our way back down the gray cobblestone streets toward the cathedral. We have read that Le Puy-en-Velay is situated among craggy volcanic outcroppings typical of the Haute-Loire region of France. A luminous statue of Our Lady sits atop a jutting volcanic peak overlooking the city as if shining her protective light on all below. She is Notre-Dame de France and is magnificent indeed. We see her as we are walking along the narrow passageways. As we walk, I ponder the idea of a divine feminine influence inserting herself into our shared cultural experience, especially in France, which is well known for its resplendent Holy Virgins and Black Madonnas. Theories abound about the significance and meaning behind these dark images of the Holy Mother and the Christ Child. Are they just ancient renderings simply blackened with age, as some propose, or are they symbols of wisdom perhaps—or something more? Whatever their origin or significance, I am anxious to see the two that I have read are housed at the Le Puy Cathedral.

Marcia and I slowly mount the long stone stairway leading up to the entrance of the cathedral. As we enter the dimly lit nave, we take our seats at the back just as the mass begins. There are a large number of pilgrims, perhaps a hundred, there for the mass and the pilgrim blessing. We all stand expectantly amid the soft glow of candles and the sweet pungent smell of incense. At the end of the mass, the priest calls the pilgrims to the front for the blessing and asks each of us to give our country of origin. We hear shouts of France, Spain, Belgium, Holland, Germany, Britain, Australia, and Japan. Marcia yells out "United States!" We laugh. We are the only ones there from the States, and we attract more attention than we want. We are both a little self conscious by now. The kindly priest passes out cheap, plastic, light blue rosaries to all. I consider it to be a precious gift.

I am anxious to see the Black Virgins. One Black Madonna is located at the front of the main sanctuary or nave. She stands cradling the little black-faced Jesus. She is clothed in a bright yellow-green robe which is encircled with a colorful array of flowers. She is crowned in stars. The other Black Madonna is tucked away in a side chapel. This one is adorned in an orange robe with silver trim. She too is cradling the Christ. I find both to be extremely interesting. To me, they represent that which is mysterious and hidden—that which is esoteric, unspoken, unacknowledged. My sister shuns them, except for their beauty as art objects, seeing them as idols that we are given admonitions not to worship. Myself, I see them as a not-so-subtle reminder of the feminine aspect of God. At the least, one cannot help but appreciate the veneration of these religious forms through the centuries. In fact, the energy in the cathedral is palpable. I can feel it.

The cathedral gift shop and bookstore is a religious spectacle all in itself. It is piled high with black virgins and St. James statues of all shapes and sizes—rosaries, souvenirs, books, and religious memorabilia. It is all rather overwhelming. I am tempted to purchase a small rendering of one of the black madonnas from the cathedral, but I think better of it and put it back. She must have whispered gently, "Let it be." After all, I would have to cram it into my backpack. "*Pas merci—absolument pas!*" No thank you—absolutely not! I have to tell myself again. This is no time for impulse buying. I decide to carry the little Black Madonna and Child in memory only and in my heart—which is about all we can do anyway in this world, in the end. I love this space of garish goods, so juxtaposed with images of the

Divine. But then I know everything is divine. So do I have to walk the Camino to be reminded of this? Apparently, I do.

A large wooden statue of St. James stands in the back of the nave. Rosaries, softly glowing votives, and boxes crammed with prayer notes have been placed on the table just at his feet. Blue plastic rosary beads are draped on him and all around him— he must be a patient sort. I imagine God smiling at all this and at us, the seekers. I wonder what manner of prayers and supplications and hopes and dreams go out as people prepare to walk the Camino. I think surely it is these repositories of faith and hope that make sites like this most holy. For me, I want to find meaning in my life beyond my day to day experience. I want rest and peace, and laughter too. I do not want to think about all the work that awaits me back at my office. *I want to unburden myself*, I think, as I hoist my heavy pack once again onto my back as we step out into the light of early morning. There must be some irony here. Maybe the deeper reason I am here will be revealed to me some day. I am hoping so.

Marcia and I retrace our steps back down the long stone stairway leading to the street below. Small figures of the Blessed Mary seem to peek out at us from the walls of houses and shops all along the narrow street. Images of Mary are everywhere, and of St. James too. We stop and get pictures of ourselves smiling and posing with a life-size wooden St. James which stands in front of one of the many lace shops. God must have laughed out loud at that. We pass by shops just beginning to open. The smell of French pastries and coffee fills the air.

We are headed for the Chapel of Saint-Michel d'Aiguilhe (Saint Michael of the Needle). This chapel, honoring St. Michael, the Archangel, was built by Bishop Godescalc after his return from his own pilgrimage to Santiago de Compostela. I was familiar with St. Michael. It has been written that he often came

Saint James at the Le Puy Cathedral of Notre Dame

Walking West on the Camino—Encore Une Fois 21

Black Madonnas at the Le Puy Cathedral

to Saint Joan of Arc in her raptures and visions prior to her sacrifice for a free France—before she was burned at the stake. And yes, we climb all 267 steps up to the chapel which sits atop a very steep rocky volcanic outcropping. We aren't counting the steps, however. We are transfixed by the beauty of our surroundings as we look down on a multitude of sparkling red clay rooftops below. We are also up front and personal with the Marian statue of Notre-Dame de France overlooking the city high on another stalagmite-shaped rock. It shines a radiant golden, deep rose color in the glow of the morning sunlight—it is exquisite. Oddly, there are two mermaids carved in stone positioned at the entrance of the chapel. They are called "the temptresses." The symbolism escapes me. Just why would they be placed way up here? I am sure it must have something to do with Eve and the apple from long ago. I don't know, maybe there is another side to it. In my practice of law these many years, I have noticed many instances of males influencing females to do bad things—burglaries, intravenous heroin use, you name it—things that I feel quite sure these women would never have dreamed up on their own had they not been, dare I say it, *tempted* by their testosterone-driven male counterparts.

We enter the dark round stone chapel and, not unsurprisingly, find a lovely statue of St. Michael. We rest for a while and take in the sweetness of the moment. Our packs are leaning up against the outer wall along with our hiking poles. We too pray for assistance as we start our journey: If I were the Camino, I would lead back to You, Oh God. Holy Spirit, keep us safe. St. Michael, protect us. St. James, guide us on the Way.

As we climb back down the steep staircase, I wonder just what it must have entailed to drag huge stones up the side of this towering volcanic peak to build the little chapel to St. Michael—and what devotion.

"God drops honey in my mouth," exclaims our new friend Kim with a wry smile as we sit around a table at his sister Annie's Cambodian restaurant. These are the folks we met on the train from Paris. We are enjoying scrumptious platters of spicy chicken dishes, savory rice, jasmine tea, and sweet Asian treats. Yes, it is easy to see why they have been so successful in their businesses. They have no time for bitterness or victim mentality—they who have opened their doors so generously to strangers like us. We see that we are already being introduced to the hospitality of the Camino. Annie, who owns this lovely restaurant, has opened her establishment to us privately for lunch. Otherwise, she is closed for the day, having just returned from their father's funeral. We marvel at their kindness. She has packed up a picnic of Cambodian sweets and leftovers for us. We thank them profusely as we head out. By now, it is almost two o'clock in the afternoon, and we are anxious to begin the Camino. We, who in our hustle-bustle Western lives rarely stop to appreciate the gifts of life in the moment, literally, the *present*. It is a true gift. The Camino is already delivering up its first of many lessons.

This early part of the Camino, leaving the town, is lined with shops selling important pilgrim things. Marcia purchases a scallop shell and attaches it to her backpack. It is a *must have* for any self-respecting pilgrim. It is similar to mine which I had purchased many years before, except hers is stamped with a small red crusader's cross. *We are now really twins*, I think to myself, with a smile, as we head out again. A warm breeze rustles the leaves on the trees as we steadily pass down the road and then into the emerald-green woods along a narrow dirt trail. We know to follow the red and white stripes which are waymarks for the GR 65. They are painted on trees, on stone fences, on sidewalks, on the sides of buildings. We see the first of them. We are on the

Chapel of Saint Michel d'Aiguilhe with Guido Reni's Michael

right path—so far so good. No thoughts, just action. It comforts me.

Nine miles in, or I should say up, we come to the Chapelle Saint-Roch, a thirteenth-century Romanesque chapel. Saint Roch is always depicted with one hand raising his mantle to show a wound on his leg which never heals. His loyal dog is at his side, the dog's mouth stuffed with bread. We read that Saint Roch has been venerated in this area of France for centuries. He is considered to be the patron saint of pilgrims. Inside, we sit at the feet of a statue of St. Roch. I can't help but ponder his legacy, particularly his faith in God, despite, and perhaps even because of, the many hardships he must have endured in his life.

My back and feet are feeling every step I take and complaining loudly. Marcia's too, she says, are whining. We agree to stay at another private gîte in Montbonnet, which is less than a mile farther. Luckily, they have beds for us. We have no ability to call and book ahead as some, we have discovered, are doing. Oh well. I seriously doubt medieval pilgrims had cell phones either. Marcia has her company phone to be used only in case of an emergency. We do not want to book ahead. We are now leaving it all to the Camino to sort out. At the gîte, we discover that we have been given single beds in an upstairs niche. Only, a young woman who is staying in the open room just below us is out very late. When she does finally show up for bed, she yells at us because we are whispering—she, who woke *us* up! Go figure. The Camino better prove itself soon, I mean, in sorting things out. Its first pick of shelter for us here has been, well, shall we say, a bit lackluster. But then, isn't this a *pilgrimage?*

After café au lait and croissants, we are out by seven o'clock this morning fairly skipping down the trail. After six miles, we stop for a rest and a water break at Rochegude at a small chapel, this one dedicated to St. James. The turreted chapel is part of the remains of an old castle and sits up on a small but steep and rocky hill. A wooden statue of St. James stands inside the chapel along with artificial pink flowers set in vases below him at the altar. It is a sweet and reverent place. We carry on and come upon a hotel-restaurant just after we pass over a bridge at the Rive Allier. It is located at the entrance to Monistrol-d'Allier. We have gone a little over eight miles. We find this charming hotel to be oh so inviting. Chairs and tables are arranged outside under bright red awnings. It is calling our names. We discover they have some rooms for pilgrims at a special pèlerin price, and we book quickly—happy to stop.

At dinner, Marcia practices her high school French, albeit with a slight Southern drawl, "*Bonsoir, Monsieur. Je voudrais un verre de vin rouge, si'l vous plait.*" She laughs at herself as she orders a glass of red wine. This is her favorite and only French sentence other than *Ca va?* roughly, how's everything? Oh, I forgot, there is one more usually directed at me: *Fermez votre bouch!* (Shut your mouth!) Oh the joys of high school French and sisters. No doubt, we feed into each other's silliness. Although we are exhausted, we are having a big time of it. If we just smile and try to speak some French and be respectful, we find that the French are kind and helpful. Of course, they always correct our bad French, but I also feel quite sure that it needs correcting. *N'est-ce pas?* We order two of those wonderful fluffy French omelets with green salads and real French dressing, not that bright orange stuff that is passed off as French dressing in our country. Back at our hotel, sleep comes early and easily for us both.

Before we know it, we are on the Camino again passing through the lovely village of Monistrol-d'Allier and then climbing up and out of the river valley. As we look back from whence we have come, the village below, nestled in the green of the valley, paints a most beautiful picture of *repose*—rest and glorious peace. It is a clear, crisp morning. *Quelle belle journée!* Yes, a beautiful day. But, the terrain is rugged and uneven as the path steeply winds its way up a small mountain. We both have collapsed on the ground for a much-needed rest and a water break. And, there she comes from behind—Leticia, our new French interpreter. She is a younger woman from Brussels who speaks good English and even better French. We met her in Le Puy earlier, and now we meet up again. Shangra la! She is as sweaty as we are, and her head is tied up in a red bandana to shield the sun. Her backpack must weigh at least forty pounds. She looks like a pack mule. We are all laughing hysterically by now. Well, why not? Who could miss the absurdity of all of *this!*

Unfortunately, the seventeenth-century Chapelle de la Madeleine, which sits deep in a grotto in the hilltop, is closed. We peer into its dark recesses through iron bars at the open windows. The chapel has been carved into the rock. Old wooden chairs are placed in front of a beautiful painting of Jesus mounted high up on the wall. In the painting, he is hanging on the cross with the three Marys kneeling below him. This must be a precious site for the community below. I picture the villagers winding their way up the mountain path in the dusky early evening, holding their candles, on their holy days. We press on together for a while and then part ways as Leticia picks up her pace. Marcia complains that I don't walk fast enough, except that I walk faster than she does going uphill. She, in turn, speeds by me when we go downhill—this is when I complain and demand she slow down. We have finally worked out a happy compromise. Did I really say *happy?* It is more of a détente. She waits for me at the bottom of a hill, and I wait for her at the top. It seems we are evenly matched this way.

As we carry on, we meet up with some more of those bovine delights who are slowly weaving their way back and forth on the country road. The Camino apparently intersects the routes back from their pastures. Who knew? We are literally hiking with the cows. Marcia and I love the cows we pass. Of course, they are usually grazing in their fenced lush, green pastures and not walking the Camino. They are such pictures of contentment. We have already earned the nickname "cowgirls" from some of our new European friends. We bid the cows *au revoir* as the Camino's red and white waymarks direct us off the road to the left and then up onto a narrow dirt trail. Soon enough, we are surrounded in dense woods and vegetation.

What we do not want to hike with are snakes (me) or chickens and roosters (Marcia). Marcia has a phobia about birds. She says she remembers a rooster flying up into her face and scratching her as a young child when we were visiting our grandmother's farm one summer in South Carolina. Now, no amount of coaxing will get her down the path if she thinks chickens are running loose nearby. We have finally worked out a plan which is about to be tested. A rooster crows loudly as we are walking down the road, approaching the village of Saugues. Marcia starts to panic. Chickens and a rooster are strutting and pecking away just ahead on the path. She spots them too. "I just can't do it," she wails. But yes, after much coaching and cajoling, Marcia closes her eyes and places her hand on my shoulder, and we gently walk together through the welcoming committee unaffected. In life, you have to do what you have to do. Me, I don't know what excuse I can give for my fear of snakes. I have resorted to referring to them as *serpents*, laughingly, since the French word evokes less anxiety for me. It is no laughing matter however. We notice a warning sign propped up on a pile of old wood in an open garage as we pass a house. It reads: *Serpents!* We steer clear and walk quickly on.

We have gone less than eight miles, but we are both ready to call it a day. My back is hurting, and my feet are refusing to proceed much farther. I am starting to get a soft blister between two toes. Marcia has no blisters as she prances along in her clunky boots. She is so sweet and, most likely, tired of me stopping so often messing around with my feet. So, she actually offers up her boots—a true sacrifice on her part. We exchange hiking boots. "*Merci beaucoup!*" I exclaim, relieved. Only now, I start to develop even more blisters in her *blister-free boots*. I decide, with a laugh, that this must be my reward for all my complaining.

We agree to stop, but where do we stay? We are in Saungues by now. Just then, our sweet friend Leticia pokes her head out of an open upstairs window yelling and waving at us with a big grin, "*Bonjour, Pèlerines!*" She directs us into the gîte she has already booked for herself. Great! We take single beds near hers and drop our packs on the floor by our beds. It is becoming a daily ritual: We unpack, layout, sort, fuss around with our things, repack, organize, take showers, wash and hang underwear and socks. If I wasn't exhausted before all this, I sure am by now. And, did I fail to mention that poor Marcia is developing a bit of a cold?

Even still, having marshaled some energy after a rest, we are both eager to check out a hiking equipment store we saw as we came into town. I want to buy a lighter weight European-style sleeping bag. I have already mailed my sleeping bag home. It was just too heavy for me to carry any longer. Plus, I sent home various other things including cooking pots, a clothes line, my mosquito head net, two pairs of socks, and my cute little travel purse. I am unable to part with my makeup, including my mascara. We have read that towards the end of the Camino, even vain city women like us throw down their mascara. That won't be *me*, I insist, much less Ms. Fancy, *Marcia*. I am hoping to take my mascara and blush across the veil some day. But I do think—

what unnecessary baggage we accumulate in life. I wish I could mail home my fear of snakes, my whining about the blisters on my feet, my occasional but entrenched negativity, not to mention those unresolved hurts over past boyfriends. Need I say more? Actually, it would be better to mail those sorts of things to the city dump. I do not want them waiting for me at my doorstep when I return—especially those boyfriend thoughts. Like years ago when Charles was irritated and screaming at me, his face contorted in a grimace, "Darling, Stand up! Stand up! Stand up!" as I was wildly whizzing past him down the ski slopes in St. Moritz, terrified, crouched down, and about to fall. It seems *release, release, release* is the order of the day on the Camino. Marcia has released things too, just not her fear of birds. I see I also am holding on to my fear of *serpents*. Oh well.

I purchase a very lightweight sleeping bag. We eat at a little restaurant close by and return to map out our next day's journey. Basically, we both calculate how far we hope to walk based on our guidebook's measurements in kilometers, village to village. Then we convert into miles multiplying by 0.62. Americans can be so tiresome. Don't get me wrong—I am happy to be one. Thus, we have a goal as to where we will spend the night, although it doesn't always work out as planned. Sometimes we stop early; sometimes we carry on farther. We are alert to guidance in such matters and to synchronicities, from whatever source they may come. I recall my early years in psychology classes. Any thoughts that, for example, the television or the radiator were speaking directly to you, were considered "ideas of reference" and a symptom of mental imbalance. So at the risk of appearing stark raving mad, I must say that it appears that the Camino is delivering up specific guidance in various forms, directly to us.

We are headed for the Domaine du Sauvage twelve miles away. The name for this region should tell us a lot. We are both a little concerned. Twelve miles may not sound like much, but we find the terrain to be rough and rugged and isolated. It is slow going. It is also beautiful. We have no sooner plopped down for a rest and a snack than we meet our soon-to-be new friends, Natalie and Emmanuel. Along they come smiling up the path. They join us for a break. On holiday and walking the Camino for only a segment, Emmanuel is trying to figure out if he should make a career change or even retire. It seems we are all trying to figure out something on the Camino. They live in the suburbs of Paris and speak some English.

We are surprised as we meet up with them again for the night at an ancient stone farmhouse at the Domaine du Sauvage. The old farm offers a *gîte* for pilgrims located in a thirteenth-century former *hospitalarie* that was established by the Knights Templars. We are grateful for it. The *gîte* has cooking facilities, along with large sticky traps filled with dead flies which are laid out on the kitchen counters. It is no bother to us. We love this ancient refuge infused with its own deep history. Leticia has stopped for the night here too. We notice she seems to be growing weary of translating for us—it is all okay. Mother would have said to us, "Don't wear out your welcome!" I am afraid we probably already have. We sit for dinner at long, massive, wooden tables where we all share pasta, cheese, bread, and red wine amid laughter and our tortured efforts to communicate back and forth. There must be twenty people from various countries booked here for the night, including us.

A word about the red wine: it is served at every pilgrim meal if you want to partake. We usually do, because a little glass of red wine offers a relaxing end to the day after a long hike. Nobody seems to abuse the privilege or drink too much, maybe because the alcohol content is less than in American wines, and also because drinking red table wine at meals is a cultural thing here—whatever. Once back home, I will return to my old ways of having an occasional glass with a friend.

"*Bonne nuit!*" I say to Natalie as we all head up the stairs to retire for the night. She gives me this funny look. I learn later that this French expression for good night is often reserved for loved ones. Or, was it my southern accent, and she had no idea what I was saying? I'll never know.

We are all out early this morning after our café au lait and bread left over from the evening before. Needless to say, we are learning to feel even more fortunate for what we have and for what we don't have. Less than two miles along, we reach another Chapelle Saint-Roch (also called the Chapelle de l'Hospitalet du Sauvage). Founded in the twelfth century, it was originally a hospital and hostel for pilgrims dedicated to St. James. It is made of huge stone blocks. Through an open iron grate, we can see a life size colorful statue of St. Roch and his dog. He is surrounded by red plastic roses and scallop shells. His pilgrim's staff in one hand, he is lifting his robe with the other to show the wound on his leg, now a familiar image to us. St. Roch, we learn, was born into a wealthy family in Montpellier in France. He later renounced his wealth and joined the Franciscans. Legend has it that he devoted himself to praying for and curing plague victims. He finally contracted the dreaded black plague himself. He is the patron saint of invalids and dogs.

Next comes Saint-Alban-sur-Limagnole, six-and-one half miles away. As we approach the village, we see fellow pilgrims sitting at tables outside a small restaurant in the main part of town. We are glad to find seats there too, and we order up a big plate of paella which we split. Of course, the best region to find this famous yellow saffron rice and seafood dish would be on the coast of Spain, but who's noticing. It is delicious. We are overjoyed to learn this lovely village has a post office. And, with much fanfare, we mail home more things. We spend the night here at a private gîte that takes donations only. Marcia wants to eat dinner here and socialize. Me, I withdraw to my bunk bed wanting solitude and rest. My lesson—not to be such a hermit next time.

Aumont-Aubrac is our destination today. It is eleven miles from St. Alban. But first, let me mention that we are now buying up cat food and dog food when we find village markets, essentials for us despite the extra weight. As we are leaving St. Alban, it is not long before we find a hungry taker—one of the village mousers. It gives us pleasure to provide a meal for a hungry kitty or dog who just happens to cross our path. Call us overly sensitive if you will, but it is such a little thing. And, I am convinced I get an endorphin rush out of it, although that is not why I do it. It is lunch on us, or should I say on God. We try not to be too obvious about our feeding escapades.

The blister between my toes has healed somewhat. I am not sure why, except that I have switched to my only other pair of socks which are thinner so that my toes have more room in my boots. Our boots, by the way, along with our hiking pants, are now caked in mud. It rained last night, and we are slogging through mud and standing water in trenches along the path. Our hiking poles are coming in handy as we poke around for shallow, less boggy places to step. Simultaneously, we wave off the bugs around our heads. "We are really having fun now, aren't we," I laugh to Marcia sarcastically. Actually, we are. No one understands the allure of the Camino unless you have walked it. "This certainly would not be *my way* of spending a vacation in Europe!" one of my friends exclaimed, with some amount of distain, before I left—she, ever the nemesis and the naysayer. I get it. But we find ourselves energized and exhilarated as we walk. It is hard to explain, although I try. We also find comfort and peace as we visit the chapels we pass along the Way. We often picnic for lunch outside by their gates or by their stone walls— lunches of canned sardines in mustard sauce, fresh tomatoes, and bread left over from our morning fare of baguettes—simple pleasures. Of course, I admit, we sometimes indulge ourselves in those naughty *croissants au chocolat*, not to mention those sweet apple pastries we find in the village *patisseries*. Oh, you poor pèlerines!

Aumont-Aubrac has a quaint village square. As we walk over to a huge hanging basket with cascading purple and white flowers, the sweet fragrance hangs heavy in the air. Nearby, a figure of Jesus on a large black iron cross forms the focal point for the village. As we head down Rue du Barry along the Camino, we find a lovely private gîte d' étape, and we are delighted to reserve two beds for the night here. It is not that we plan for or seek out these private gîtes. We are also bunking in municipally run facilities, when we can, which we find quite adequate. It is just that this one is again calling our names. We are quite fortunate for it, too, because we find ourselves seated at dinner at a crowded table where platters are piled high with this most heavenly concoction of *aligot* and green salads. Our smiling host and his gracious wife have prepared steaming piles of mashed potatoes with garlic butter and melted local white cheese, a regional favorite they call "*aligot*." It is dished out in long, stringy, heavenly helpings onto our plates. Excitement runs high. *"Bon appetit!"* someone exclaims, as we lift our glasses of red wine high and toast our hosts and their beautifully prepared meal. I practice my French slowly and in a halting manner at the table. Someone even points out to my sister that I am, indeed, speaking somewhat intelligible *français*. That same friend from home once said that she was "not a linguist." It was a not-so-subtle way of letting me know, neither am I, so why am I studying French? This is a foregone conclusion I cannot contest. But I am pleased to try, and isn't this what matters at the end of the day? Trolls under the bridge only propel me to pick up my pace.

We have fallen again into the sublime and simple rhythms of the Camino. This morning, we have stopped in several churches, including one in La Chaze-du-Peyre. The old church has a beautiful, round, stained glass window of the Virgin Mary behind the choir loft. As we turn to leave, we look up to find this sublime surprise. As we proceed, our walking guide alerts us that we are about to cross the Aubrac Plateau and to expect temperatures to drop. So, we bundle up. I should say layer up. By nightfall we end up at a farm that does meals for pilgrims and maintains a gîte, the beautiful Ferme des Gentianes. An iron sculpture of a cow's head is proudly hung over the mantle in the dining room—another reminder that this region is cow country in the high plateau. Today, we have done almost ten miles—it is plenty.

I had already hiked this vast range of rocky high country and pasture lands in 1999. Gray stones and boulders are piled high to form fences along the path. All manner of yellow and blue wild flowers—daffodils and narcissus—and grasses line the dirt trail. As we climb, we can see for miles on the high plateau. I remember this wild green section as one of the most spectacular points on the Camino. It does not disappoint this second time around. Marcia is awed, too. We meet up again with our friend Leticia, who is by now contemplating going home. The Camino is taking its toll on her.

We finally stop at a village market in Nasbinals and stock up on more cat food and drinking water. A large stone statue of a pilgrim stands outside the shop. An iron bust of one, Pierre Brioude, along with a pair of iron crutches, stands across the way in the square. He was the one tasked with setting broken bones. I wonder just how many poor pilgrims broke ankles and limbs on this path. Apparently, more than a few! Business must have been booming. We walk across the street to the church. The facade at the altar is a stunning mint green and gold. It fairly glows behind various statues of the saints. A statue of Mary stands at the center—behind her head, a large scallop shell.

We have forgotten the significance of the shell and sit for awhile to see what we might read about it. The scallop shell is one of the iconic symbols of the Camino. It is *coquille Saint Jacques* in French. The shell itself, with its fractal-like natural design, forms the many routes pointing to Santiago de Compostela. It is thought that the shell may have been a feminine fertility symbol in the early Celtic traditions. Another theory is that it represents the sun setting in the west behind the sea, symbolizing death and then resurrection. So it is, perhaps, not by accident that we walk west on the Camino—death to the old and then rebirth and renewal. Legend has it that St. James himself saved a certain drowned knight who then rose up out of the water covered in *coquilles*—fascinating. The symbol of the scallop shell is everywhere. We have even noticed that as we walk through certain larger towns on the Camino, the scallop shell is impressed in brass into the sidewalks at our feet. Look up or look down to find your way—you choose.

We turn our attention back to our lunch. We are sitting in the grass by the church, our backpacks staring intently at us. They are propped up on a wall nearby. We are having a *déjeuner* of ham and cheese sandwiches and potato chips. We notice happily that we are not gaining weight although we are often eating big portions of carbohydrates like pasta and potatoes. We are losing weight. It occurs to me that it would be easier to find some other diet plan than to walk the high Aubrac plateau—I'm just saying.

I distinctly remember the cows in their straw bonnets, flower garlands, and cowbells I saw when I was in this area many years ago. I am expecting and hoping to see them again, only to learn that we had come along unawares on the very day of the yearly spring festival in Aubrac back then. It would be like winning the lottery—one in three hundred and sixty-five chances. The festival occurs always the third Sunday in May. We had just happened to be there on their big festival day. I didn't realize the synchronicity at the time. So, no cow bonnets today, unfortunately for us. But, we hear the melodic tinkling of cowbells occasionally mixed in the rustle of the breeze as we pass these beautiful cows grazing lazily in their pastures. Cowbells hang on some of their necks. They are, after all, the true "cowgirls."

We are looking ahead for the village of Aubrac. We have come almost thirteen miles, a lot of it uphill, across the plateau. The waymark painted on a tree points us left down a narrow, grassy, dirt path by a modern sculpture. Marcia and I are praying to find a good place to eat and to rest our heads for the night here. It is getting late in the afternoon, and we are both tired and longing to take off our boots—even Marcia. And, like a miraculous vision, up rides a dashing old gentleman on a magnificent prancing and pawing white horse, an equally handsome black steed trailing behind him. He asks us if we would like to dine at his *gîte* this evening. He also directs us up to the road to the central part of the village to a facility which houses pilgrims. We feel blessed. We suspect the locals, including this kind fellow, look out for the *pèlerins* (French for pilgrims) who are approaching their village to offer help—not unlike the help their ancestors offered here in the Middle Ages.

Now, I remember this charming village as we round the corner of one of the buildings and find the lovely restaurant, Chez Germaine, on the village square. Large colorful fruit tarts are laid out in the windows. *No wonder I have been plotting my way back to the Camino*, I think to myself. We had eaten lunch here many years before. And, did I mention, we had also ordered up slices of that luscious tart. We make a mental note to return *tout de suite* (right away) as soon as we can find beds for the night.

Marcia and I manage to reserve spaces at La Grange d'Aubrac Refuge, the place our dashing horseman had recommended. This gîte is located in an ancient stone building, a former hospital for pilgrims. The *Domerie* was founded by a Flemish knight named Adelard de Flandres. He had needed refuge here while on the Camino, having been waylaid by thieves. We climb massive stone stairs winding up a high tower to our room. There are eight bunk beds lined up along the stone walls. We take two beds on the bottom bunks and arrange our things. There are heavy woolen blankets set out on every bed.

The window sash is open. We can feel the coolness of the evening approaching quickly—we are relieved to be here.

Heading back to the restaurant, we happen to meet up with two new friends from Norway who are also walking the Camino. They are basking in the late afternoon sun at tables set up outside, enjoying their glasses of wine. We join them and order up one huge slice of that raspberry tart, which we split. Across the street in the village square, the self-appointed greeter and mascot for the village, a huge St. Bernard, is standing in a water trough cooling off. He clearly doesn't need our dog food. This friendly mutt just wants to get his belly rubbed. Of course, we oblige him. We head back to our room, now booked full, along with the rest of the facility. We feel fortunate. Pilgrims are being turned away.

The *Domerie* sits just next to the twelfth-century Church of Notre-Dame des Pauvres. This church and its refuge was home to the monks and the knights of the Order of Aubrac until the French Revolution. Inside the old church, there are rows and rows of wooden chairs set out before statues of Jesus and the Blessed Mary. The soft glow of the candlelight and the smell of incense invite us to linger for a long while. There are all sorts of paper prayers taped on the walls at the back of the church, including this message painted in red: *"Jésus s'approache et fit route avec eau."* Luke 24:15. Literally, Jesus approaches and makes a way with them. I write it down to look it up later in the King James Bible: "Jesus himself drew near, and went with them." *Oh, that Jesus would walk with me*, I muse to myself.

For now, we have an appointment to keep for dinner at the stable of that kind old gentleman who rode up and greeted us on his horse. As we sit at his long wooden table inside his stable, we learn he had been an attorney, but had long since given up the practice of law to live his life *his way* and to tend to the pilgrims. He lives in a village nearby and comes over to Aubrac daily to care for his horses and the pèlerins. A large caldron of broth is bubbling on his old stove. Coarse bread is set out and, of course, le vin rouge. There are others at his table too. As I look back, I consider this occasion to rank as one of the most moving and special experiences in my life—bar none.

We go home early to our bottom bunks and those warm wool blankets. We need them this night. We figure the Europeans must like their cold nights, as the windows are left open all night long. Adding to the ambience, a fellow pilgrim has gotten in late and climbs into the top bunk across from me and is soon adding a chorus of snores to the mix. Others are awake by now, and we snicker and joke out loud to signal our shared misery. The man doesn't wake up or stop his snorts. I sleep in all the clothes I brought with me and still shiver in my bed. My cold nose is barely sticking out from the blanket until, finally, I nod off to sleep exhausted. This is another day that has gone exceptionally well on the Camino, except for all the snoring.

Of course, we are up and out early this morning. Some of our fellow pilgrims got up even earlier, when it was still dark. They packed up and left quickly with headlights on. *Why?* I wonder. They will miss out on the spectacular views leaving the village. This morning, however, the fog hangs low as we leave. It is still eerily beautiful and otherworldly. We munch on our protein bars that we brought from home, anticipating a stop for coffee at Saint-Chély-d'Aubrac. It is almost five miles away; we are anxious to get there. We stop at the first open café we see in St. Chély for café au lait. A life size brown sculpture of a cow stands in the middle of the picturesque village square. We then walk across the street to their fifteenth-century cathedral. Inside, we find a lovely statue of St. Roch and his dog as well as those of St. Francis of Assisi and Jesus. Jesus is clothed in a red and white robe that glitters with gold. A beautiful painting of the Blessed Mary hangs on the wall in a side chamber. Her hands are outstretched in the ascension. Her sacred heart blazes in red against her white gown and dark blue robe. Cherubs around her feet gaze up at her.

Marcia and I love these ancient churches and cathedrals we pass along the Camino. This one is unusually beautiful. We notice that some pilgrims do not go in. I assume they walk the Camino in a secular way or a Zen way, or perhaps wanting to be free of organized religion. There is certainly something to be said for detachment and non-grasping. But, there is a particular beauty and even majesty these old churches represent in the effort of humanity to approach the Divine. A feeling of devotion and hope fairly seeps through the walls.—enough of that for now.

We leave the cathedral, hoist our backpacks onto our backs yet again, snap up our hiking poles, rearrange our wide-brimmed hats, put on sunscreen, and carry on. Oh, the modern pilgrim! I have to laugh. Staying in the moment, I notice, is a very good thing. The Camino asks that of us, to be alert to what the *now* brings. No telephone calls, no text messages, no pesky emails—I like it a lot. I feel more grounded. We walk down a narrow road lined with lavender hydrangea bushes, what we called snowball bushes as children. We cross an old stone bridge leaving town, climb uphill on the path, and then turn to look back down over the village, tucked into the green valley below.

We are setting our sights for Saint-Côme d'Olt. From Aubrac, we will have walked a little over seventeen miles. *Ça suffit!* Yes, it is quite enough. I am reminded of what an old friend of mine from Mississippi had to say about that popular French phrase. With a gentle smile, she tells a story about her older sister. Her sister fancies herself to be more sophisticated, having dated Elvis a few times, and she being the oldest too. She always ends a big Southern meal, such as fried chicken and collard greens, with *ça suffit!* Or, as my friend translates in English, "This is sufficient!" It is certainly not the typical boorish announcement of "I'm full!" Oops! I must have walked down that route not noticing the X mark on the tree. I diverted on a tangent, but a fun one since that French expression is indelibly marked on my brain after my friend's tale about her sister and now, most likely, on yours too.

Back on the Camino, we notice that we are growing stronger and are able to walk farther with fewer complaints from our backs and feet, a small miracle all in itself. At the entrance to Saint-Côme, we come upon signs for a convent just up the road on the right and slightly off the path. We seriously weigh the idea of trudging over there. Any diversion off the Camino has to be carefully considered, and our feet have to be consulted. The answer is a resounding *yea* for both of us. I am so glad it is, since we end up staying at the large Couvent de Malet, which provides some accommodations for pilgrims. For about thirty-five dollars, we book a simple room with two single beds and a private bathroom, dinner, and petit déjeuner for the next morning. To be sure, this convent is another welcoming oasis on the Way of St. James.

As we leave early this morning, we notice a lovely large white statue of Mary and the Baby Jesus which stands in the lush gardens by the convent. We retrace our steps slightly to get back on the Camino and head into Saint-Côme d'Olt. It is considered to be one of the most beautiful medieval villages in France. Our guidebook tells us that *Olt* is the old name for the Lot River. We stop for a while at their sixteenth-century church. Magnificent, long, shimmering, stained glass windows line the church walls inside. A large wooden cross with a figure of Jesus stands at the altar at the front. The nave glows a rosy gold in the subdued light. We are awed once more. As we turn to leave, an exquisite rose window shines forth from the church balcony. We cross an ancient stone bridge over the River Lot and press on towards Espalion which, we anticipate, is not far away.

Espalion is a large town which bustles with all kinds of shops and activity. We nose in and out of the shops for a while and end up quarreling over what to do next. Marcia and I get

The Église de Saint-Pierre-de-Bessuéjouls

along well together—until we don't. This is one of those moments. At the least, we agree to carry on. We hurry through the busy area and cross a large pilgrim bridge over the Lot River to head out of town. We have a stride going, except that now Marcia is walking much faster than I am. She is also irritated I am swinging my hiking poles in a different way than she does and, she says, most hikers do. I am apparently not getting the traction I need to go faster. Finally, not without some amount of irritation, I tell her, "Go on without me. I must walk at my own pace and swing my poles *my way!*" It is another metaphor for life, I guess. "No nooooo!" she says. You are getting the picture as to how this morning is unfolding. At some point, we may want to walk separately. But really, we mostly like each other and enjoy our time together. *D'accord!* Okay, we agree to carry on *ensemble*.

Almost two miles later, we reach the Église de Saint-Pierre-de-Bessuéjouls, one of the oldest churches on the Camino. I remember this beautiful church. I had been here before on my second pilgrim trip back in 1999. A painting, so hauntingly lovely, still hangs on one of the walls on the first floor. A shepherd girl, tending her sheep, is being visited by an angel from above who is handing her a red rose. I wonder if this pretty innocent young girl is Saint Joan of Arc? I am a fan of Joan's and have recently read and greatly enjoyed Mark Twain's book about her. As I gaze at the painting again, I wonder if Joan knew what was in store for her as she answered the call to lead the disorganized and demoralized French troops into battle, ultimately, driving the British out of France. In 1431, at the height of The Hundred Years War, she was burned at the stake for heresy and witchcraft, claims that later proved to be false. She is now venerated as a martyr, oddly enough, by the same Catholic Church that played a big part in seeing her executed. There is so much rich history and contradiction to contemplate.

We wind up the old stone stairway in the bell tower to the eleventh-century chapel dedicated to St. Michael. On up, and we stand at the top of the tower. We have a great view of the countryside, with its sparkling green meadows and farmland. In the tower, we can see the remains of what look like Celtic knot designs and angels carved into the pillars, remnants of bygone days. A cold breeze wafting through the tower window reminds us it is time to leave. Neither of us really wants to go—it is all so sublime.

We pass through several hamlets. In one, an old church is open, and it has a statue of St. Michael slaying the dragon, symbolizing Satan. *St. Michel* is dressed in aqua blue and gold. We rest here for just a little while. The Camino then takes us down a paved road which gives us an opportunity to make more time, until the waymarks suddenly direct us up a steep wooded hill on a very narrow dirt footpath. *What next?* The Camino asks many things of us—a big one is that we be flexible. *Go with the flow* takes on a whole new meaning here. Mostly, I go peacefully. But other times, I go with some amount of irritation. When, in a rare moment, I can catch myself, I notice that the Camino just may be serving up something different or even better than we ever expected. Then, it becomes a walk of faith and wonder. If it is predictability you crave, better to check in at your trusty timeshare in Mexico. Marcia snaps a picture of me from behind struggling straight up a very steep, narrow path through the woods. I am leaning forward into the climb, letting the weight of my backpack propel me forward. Or, should I say, I am humped over by that pack of mine, it yelling out commands that I carry on—like I am some pack animal. No one will believe this latest diversion. We can hardly believe it ourselves. We eventually wind back down onto a dirt road and then a paved road out of the woods again.

And here, we are pleasantly surprised to see that the beautiful town of Estaing looms just across the Lot River in front of us in the hills. Estaing, we have read, is another village listed as one of the *plus beaux villages* of France. The sun casts bands of prism-colored light onto the river and the village just beyond. We stop for more pictures and then enter Estaing, crossing a

Rue du College in Estaing

magnificent ancient stone bridge. The fifteenth-century church of Saint Fleuret sits glowing in the sunshine on the horizon high above the town. Having come almost eleven miles, we want to stop for the day.

We are looking for 8 Rue du College where we hope to find pilgrim lodging. To our delight, it is July 1 and the *fête* (festival day) honoring St. Fleuret. This is another lottery win for us. Not to say that I think anything is an accident in this world. I cringe when I think what could have gone wrong if we had actually tried to plan this. Lesson here—the universe often serves up such amazing surprises if you just don't try to control things so much, if you don't plan so much, if you just relax and let go. That is easier said than done. Young people are dancing in the streets in medieval village costumes in front of a restaurant with a blue awning which reads: *"Bienvenue aux pèlerins!"* (Welcome to the pilgrims!) A local band is playing polka tunes. There are colorful flags and banners strung up all around. Our friends from Norway are seated outside at a nearby restaurant enjoying the festivities. We sit for a while with them. They had called ahead and booked at a small hotel on the square. This was a wise move.

Marcia and I, who are by now receiving daily lessons in trust (and failing that lesson this very moment), are starting to get a little anxious about where we can find beds for the night, especially since it is festival time and the weekend. The Camino seems to be a condensed metaphor for life. Maybe we are noticing this because we walk everywhere. Time is not speeding by down the freeway. And need I say it, neither are we. The sun is sinking fast, and so we hurriedly make our way up the cobblestone streets toward the church looking for Rue du College. We are winding in and out of narrow passageways. We have figured out that, often, pilgrim accommodations can be found near the church which is the focal point for the village—if those gîtes are not booked solid, that is. We finally locate the College and before we can even rap on the massive wooden door at number 8, we hear footsteps. Out front, a flat gray slab painted in white letters reads: "*Hospitalité St Jacques-Accueil Pèlerins*," meaning roughly "pilgrim home." Sign us right up! Pots of bright red geraniums line the doorway. A most cheerful woman opens the door wide and greets us with a broad smile and a big b*onsoir*, almost as if anticipating our arrival. I practice my French, *"Bonsoir, Madame. Comment allez-vous? Est-ce que vous avez des lits pour ce soir?"* I am getting better at this, although my favorite French expression is still *"Je ne sais pas. Parlez-vous englais?"* It means "I don't know. Do you speak English?" We are hoping that she, indeed, has some beds for us this night.

As divine timing would have it, dinner is just being served. And, there are spaces for us at the table and beds for the night. They are the last ones. *Voilà!* Oh, ye of little faith! We feel like we truly have come home. We drop our bags inside the door for now and take our seats at a long table just off the open kitchen. Large steaming pies of quiche lorraine and fresh butter-lettuce green salad are the order of the evening meal, as well as sliced baguettes from the local market and a citrus tart for desert. Our hosts (volunteers for the summer) are so kind and gracious, bustling around serving dinner.

Afterwards, I gather up my last vestiges of energy and hurriedly make my way further up the cobblestone street to the Church of St. Fleuret, hoping to catch mass. I do not want to miss out on anything. This is a gorgeous old church that has been well preserved. The local parishioners are tolerant, it seems, of us pilgrims who drop in occasionally to their mass. There are several pilgrims besides me attending tonight. Of course, the mass is said in French. I do not understand much of it. What I *do*, however, understand is their devotion and deep serenity. And, the beauty of the cathedral eclipses everything else. The nave is adorned in gold and green and decorated with dazzling paintings of the saints, Mary, and Jesus. A mosaic pattern of a large heart has been set into the cobbled street at the back entrance. St Fleuret is the patron saint of Estaing. He is credited for converting the village to Christianity on his way, winning souls, through the Aveyron region of France, in the Midi-Pyrenees. It is believed he died in 621. A beautiful gold statue of the saint stands in the church near the front altar. It is clear the parishioners love their patron saint. After mass, I rush *home* intending to stretch out on my bunk and to map out our next day's adventure, only to fall fast asleep. If there was any snoring going on near me, I missed it all.

This morning, we have to backtrack across the bridge to regain the Camino. Not a problem, since the early morning sunshine makes the geraniums blaze bright red and pink against the blue sky. This is one time I don't mind retracing my steps—it is all so lovely. It is on to Golinhac, almost ten miles away. We read there are two municipal gîtes d' étape there, and we are hoping to find beds at one of them. July is a busy season on the Camino. Sure enough, the gîtes in town are completely full. We have already been coaching ourselves to expect a miracle. After some amount of thought and tortured conversation back and forth, Madame, at one of the overflowing gîtes, hands us keys to the *gîte équestre*, situated less than a mile back just before Golinac in the hamlet of Le Radal. We fairly skip back down the road to our destination so excited to find beds are we. Tra la la! This is another time we don't mind heading back. The facility is a very old two-story stone building with a slate roof, characteristic of the region. A stable is attached for horses. The kitchen is neat and clean, and stuffed chairs are arranged around a beautiful old fireplace in the great room. We climb the stairs to the sleeping quarters where five bunk beds line up along brightly painted yellow walls. We end up with a private house for the night. No one else books here but us. We pay forty dollars for beds, dinner at their local restaurant, and petit déjeuner—unbelievable. The Camino, we observe firsthand, is a better travel agent than we ever expected. It has sorted out a lot for us. We unpack, shower, and repack. You know the drill.

We then make it a point to visit the church of Saint Martin in the village; it is the only structure that remains of a ninth-century Benedictine abbey. Inside, we find another lovely statue of St. Roch, dressed in a dark pilgrim cape and hat decorated with scallop shells, his dog at his side. He carries a staff and gourd, another now familiar symbol on the Camino. Gourds were used to carry water in medieval times. Much to our delight, at dinner, we meet up with a young American couple. Marcia and I sit family style at a large table with fellow pilgrims and share our experiences of the Camino. After dinner, we are tired and walk back to our gîte in the dusk of early evening, marveling at the day.

We drop by this same charming restaurant for café au lait and croissants this morning on our way heading out of town. The Camino is unusually beautiful along this next stretch. We are walking down a narrow asphalt road by split rail fences and colorful fields of wildflowers. We walk in and out of wooded areas, by pastures, and then pass through several hamlets. Red geraniums in pots and purple and pink hydrangea bushes seem to wave and call out *bonjour* everywhere we look. We meet up with a Belgium man who is walking by himself. He is faster than we are. As we wave him on, he chatters merrily about the French and their fondness for the names of their villages—all ending in "ac." And yes, we then turn right slightly off the path to visit the Church of Saint Pierre in Espeyrac. We have come almost six miles. Inside the church, there is a beautiful rendition in stained glass of Jesus with outstretched hands. A large statue of Mary, dressed in different hues of blue, stands in an alcove painted gold. Gold *fleurs-de-lis* shine like stars on the pale blue walls around her, amid statues of Saint Peter and St. Roch. We, who have already dropped our backpacks and poles way behind us by the detour to the church, sink into the pews to rest our weary feet and to take it all in. About the *fleur-de-lis* (literally, flower of the lily): I know it signifies French royalty, but what else? This three-petal stylized design is an ancient symbol that has appeared across cultures and time. In Christendom, it is an emblem of the Blessed Mary as well as of the Trinity. We often see them painted in gold in these old churches and cathedrals—they blaze like stars across ceilings of azure or aqua.

As we head out, we reclaim our packs and hiking poles. Neither of us seems to worry about someone taking our pèlerin things or theft on the Camino. After all, who would want our stuff but *us*? In my wildest fantasy, I see myself flinging my backpack as far away as I can, as I run screaming down the Camino, free at last. I think we are all seeking some form of freedom as we experience the Camino, just probably not that kind. There are shuttle services that haul pilgrim luggage by van to the appointed destination or gîte for the night. I guess that is fair game for those who book ahead and cannot physically bear the weight, as well as for those who are older and are lucky just to get *themselves* down the path. We are not tempted to use a shuttle service, so far.

We pass through several hamlets and then reach Sénergues, a beautiful medieval village with its turreted castles and church of St. Martin. Inside the church, we find another statue of St. Roch with two cherub faces at its base. Lovely modern stained glass windows bedazzle the dimly lit sanctuary with streams of orange and yellow light. We leave this lovely church and village and climb steeply uphill and through woods until we reach a plateau of pasture lands. Marcia helps me dig apples out of my bag, and we feed some curious mules who are poking their heads around the barbed wire fence to greet us. We snap more pictures—we are fond of the mules too. We finally reach the Church of Saint-Marcel. Saint Marcel, a pope, was martyred in the early fourth century. This church once served as a leprosarium. At the worst outbreak of the plague, it was a chapel dedicated to St. Roch.

We have walked almost fourteen miles when, by late afternoon, we reach Conques. Conques is another one of *les plus*

"Mystical Rose" at Abbaye Saint-Foy in Conques

beaux villages in France. It is lightly drizzling, and we have stopped several times, most recently, to retrieve our rain capes out of our backpacks. Despite the rain, a kindly priest is standing in the middle of the narrow cobblestone street at the bridge entering Conques directing us left and then down to the Accueil Abbaye Saint-Foy. This three-story abbey maintains a large dormitory for pilgrims. It sits just behind the magnificent Romanesque Cathedral of Saint-Foy. Pink hollyhocks line the narrow concrete walkway down to it. The Abbey shines fairly purple in the mist. We are greeted by empty stone caskets which are open and laid out in the grass behind the cathedral just across from the abbey—a macabre sight, I must say. This is a large pilgrim refuge. Even so, we are lucky to find beds. For thirty dollars, we have reserved beds, dinner, and petit déjeuner. We wind our way up massive spiral stone steps to our assigned places. There are rows of bunk beds on both walls in a large rectangular room. It is co-ed, of course, although the showers and bathrooms are segregated. It is getting cool and we hurriedly shower and go back down for dinner.

Their large dining room is cozy and inviting. We are seated with pilgrims from across Europe, including our friends from Norway and Belgium who are also staying here. We are excited to see them—it is a reunion of sorts. Marcia and I seem to be the only Americans and are a novelty act once again. Gracious indeed are our many hosts. They are mostly lay volunteers. We are served four courses. The French know how to do it right. Baskets of sliced baguettes are passed around the table, as well as water and red wine, for those who want it. After dinner, we head for bed. I have the luck of the draw—the top bunk. Getting in and out of top bunks is a little tricky for us, especially in the dark and in the middle of the night, but we manage. I keep my trusty little flashlight close by me on my bed for just such occasions. Sleep comes easily. We are fortunate to be able to book a second night at the abbey. We want to rest a day and just be tourists here in beautiful Conques. And, we want to wander in and out of the

Chapelle Saint-Roch, near the village of Noailhac

shops and restaurants and the cathedral and its museum nearby—*sans* backpacks.

The Abbey Church of Saint Foy (Faith) has its roots in the eighth century, although the current cathedral was built three centuries later. Saint Foy, a teenage girl, was martyred in AD 303. Her relics attracted much attention to the cathedral, as she was believed to be able to cure eye ailments. As we enter the cathedral, we can't help but notice the Tympanum of the Last Judgment with its graphic depiction of some unfortunate souls being eaten or bludgeoned by gleeful demons, while other more fortunate souls are being lovingly helped by angels from above. Let's see, which do I choose? The church is dimly lit with candles. The sweet smell of incense wafts in the air. Hikers are crowded at the front by the altar participating in the pilgrim mass. We join them quickly for the prayer.

Conques is situated in a basin surrounded by wooded mountains. The village itself is built on several levels with stone stairs leading to higher or lower sections of the town. We climb one of the stairways to reach the higher section. The two steeple spires of the cathedral loom large over the valley and form a reference point for us as we set out to explore the village. It is a beautiful day. The sky has cleared nicely. Orange trumpet vines hang heavy on the old walls and fences. Bright red geraniums decorate window boxes and pots everywhere we look. A white kitty is stretched out sunning herself on a window sill. We walk the length of the village and climb a rocky hill hoping to visit the Chapelle Saint-Roch. Unfortunately, it is closed, but it affords us a beautiful view of the surrounding area.

Marcia and I treat ourselves to pizza and green salads for lunch outside at a quaint restaurant in the central part of town. We also buy tickets and take in the abbey museum which houses the jeweled gold reliquary statue, the Majesty of Saint Foy, as well as artifacts from the cathedral. Marcia buys a beautiful gold

Walking West on the Camino—Encore Une Fois 55

shell pendant from one of the shops. Tourist status is fun for us this day. By day's end, we enjoy another lovely dinner at the abbey and then walk around to the church just as the sun is setting low on the purple horizon. We are eager to attend mass, as well as a special organ concert and light show extravaganza given every evening in the summer months. At the grand finale, the priest bangs out "The House of the Rising Sun"—a fitting, rather surreal choice of music for the occasion. As we step out into the evening dusk, the cathedral spires glow fiery red against the backdrop of the dark purple sky. Returning the short distance to our *abbey home*, Marcia presents me with a CD of the organ music that she purchased from the gift shop, unbeknownst to me. It is a sweet remembrance of our time in beautiful Conques.

More rested, we press on again in the early morning haze. We retrace our steps, traversing the village again down Rue Charlemagne, as we head out onto the Camino. We pass by the picturesque Auberge Du Pont Romain which is just by the old bridge before we cross over the Rive Dourdou leaving town. The auberge is an inviting spot with its lovely red awnings and tables and chairs set outside, the smell of coffee and freshly baked baguettes and croissants in the air. We are literally climbing up and out—it is tough going. We reach the little stone Chapelle Saint-Foy, which is perched on a rocky outcrop half way up the side of the mountain overlooking Conques. It affords a gorgeous view of the village below. We have climbed almost a mile on a narrow, wooded, winding, steep trail. We have to stop frequently to rest. This chapel, dedicated to St. Foy, is a pilgrim destination for the locals all in itself. Inside, we find a lovely statue of the girl, Saint Foy. Votives and pink flowers are set out below her. There is also a beautiful stained glass window of the pilgrim, St. James. We each take our turn and ring the church bell which tolls its soulful melody across the valley. I just think lots of angels must be getting their wings right about now. Why, it must be a full time job for some of them, just traveling the Camino with us! A bubbling brook by the chapel is reputed to be a healing spring for those with eye ailments. We tarry here for awhile and rest. After all, the sound of the brook is music to the soul.

Again, we climb steeply uphill—it is rough and slow going still. The forested path is fairly soggy from all the rain. I remember this area from when I walked here many years ago before turning back. We regretfully had run out of time and had to return to the States. I had so much wanted to go on up this beautiful path. Now I can. I also think of those many little black leeches we saw right in this location on my first time here. Or were they just slugs? It's more fun for me to think they were leeches. None are around today. *C'est dommage!* Yes, it is a pity! It is not often that I encounter a leech—of course, unless it is the human variety, that is, or should I say an *energy vampire*. You know the ones—those who drain your energy with negativity or constant chatter.

We walk through the village of Noailhac and soon reach the lovely Chapelle Saint-Roch just beyond. Here, the locals come to celebrate St. Roch's Day, on August 16th. We discover strikingly beautiful modern stained glass windows inside with swirling patterns of pink and purple and blue and orange. They look like bursts of sparkling fireworks lighting up the sky. There are two statues of St. Roch, one above the door into the chapel, and another at the altar.

Decazeville is almost seven miles away, so we carry on. This is a sizeable community. It takes us quite a while to walk through, first the commercial district, and then the suburbs. By now, I am complaining about my feet once more. The blister between my toes has returned. As usual, Marcia has no blisters at all. So, we take a break and eat our picnic lunch just off the road in the grass. We are having mustard sardines again, fresh tomatoes, and slices of bread left over from breakfast. And, a little black and white kitty is enjoying some cat food Marcia has retrieved from her backpack. I have to take off my boots and allow my feet to breathe for awhile. I will not be whining around to wear Marcia's boots again, however. Am I an *energy vampire* right about now? Well, if the shoe fits…

We stop at another Église Saint-Roch next, a little over a mile past Decazeville. The rounded ceiling of this parish church is painted sky blue. There is an image of Jesus as the Master with angels at his feet in the clouds. A statue of St. James stands in a recess behind the front altar, a statue of Mary on the wall nearby. This is a perfect place for us to rest our feet again and reflect on our journey.

As we press on, the Camino continues across rolling hills and pasturelands. We pass beautiful dark brown horses with white tails and manes grazing in their pastures. They look up curiously. Some speak as we walk by them. Round bales of hay sit ready in the fields. Then, we head up a steep, rocky, narrow path. Our hiking poles are coming in handy again for traction. We also have to grab the branches of trees that are extending their leafy arms, so that we can propel ourselves up—it is *that* steep. We finally reach the village of Livinhac-le-Haut and find bunk beds at a gîte d' étape. We have come fifteen miles this day—plenty. This facility has a kitchen, where we cook up pasta and canned tomato sauce for dinner and then head for our beds and sleep land. Those clouds from the Eglise Saint-Roch swirl in my thoughts, until I am able to catch one and float gently away.

Early this morning, we stop at the local patisserie for our usual café au lait and croissants and move on in the direction of Figeac, our target city for the day. It is another fifteen miles away. We pass through Montredon with its two beautiful churches and also walk two or three quiet hamlets. We have read we can bypass the scenic route and, alternatively, head straight for the village of Saint Félix. But, somehow, we miss this more direct route and are winding our way ad infinitum by fields and finally by a reservoir we had hoped to bypass. By now, we are discovering our error, and I sit down to have a meltdown. I mean it. I am irritated and complaining and generally acting badly—so much for going with the flow. Marcia is doing better than I am, to her credit, but her feet don't have blisters either. *No excuses!* Then, feeling even more sorry for myself, I start in on a tearful tangent about how we continually pray for help and guidance, and so what happened here?

But then, up pop our Parisienne friends, Natalie and Emmanuel. We see them in the distance walking toward us from whence we came. Had we taken the shorter, more direct route, we would have missed them entirely. Enough said, except one last comment: *Call it all good*. They are as surprised to run into us as we are of them. They had actually taken two or three days off of the Camino to check in on a family member who had taken ill near Paris. We laughingly rest and drink water, all of us collapsed in the grass like wet noodles. Looking across to a pasture, Marcia comments on the sublime beauty of sheep grazing in the distance. She is an especially big fan of sheep, partly because she loves the Great Shepherd, and also because *she*, ever the artist, likes to paint them. So much of our time near sheep consists of her staying way too long to snap photos of them and me hurrying us on. I make a mental note not to be so controlling next time. I think I am pretty patient, until I am not.

All walking together, we reach Saint Félix and the Romanesque Church of Saint Radegonde. An eleventh-century stone carving of Adam and Eve and the serpent, wrapped around the tree of life, forms the tympanum at the entryway to the church. There are colorful stained glass windows of Mary and of Saint James, as well as a beautiful old painting of Our Lady of Sorrows. A painting of Jesus recreated from the image on the Shroud of Turin hangs on another wall. This church is too lovely for words. We part ways again with our friends who are pressing on faster than we are.

As we leave the village, the Camino literally takes us on a dirt path between an old stone building and a tall, ivy-covered wall. Maybe the passageway is three feet wide if we are lucky. As we squeeze through, I am regretting all those croissants, not to mention the apple tarts, I have been eating. Marcia snaps a picture of me from behind—me, ever vigilant for serpents as we tread these grassy little suspect paths. We continue past rolling pastures and fields. Barbed wire fences are surrounded by tall grass, white Queen Anne's lace, and goldenrod. It is nature's summer bouquet and *la joie de vivre!* Yes, we can both feel it as we walk—exhilaration and joy and the beauty of this moment lifting our spirits high.

We reach the Église de Saint Mirabel, another stunning Romanesque church along the Way. Inside, there is a striking stained glass window of St. Germaine who is clothed in blue and green robes. The brick interior of this church shines a warm orange-red hue as sunlight from a high small window illuminates the altar. A fairly glowing Jesus figure hangs on the cross in the subdued light. Again, we sit and practice the beautiful *now*.

We are anxious to get to Figeac, since it is closing in on early evening and we want to secure beds for the night. Figeac is a very large town on the River Célé complete with rail and bus services. Once there, we anxiously try to find beds at several *gîtes* with no luck. We retrace our steps back up the street and then come across an old stone house with a brightly painted blue door. Two pilgrim boots full of flowers are balanced on a ledge above the door. A scallop shell hangs on the door frame—our kind of place! Fortunately, we get the last two beds, which are situated in a private room on the top level of the house. We share a bathroom with others. *Pas de problème!* Why argue with the Camino? After we spread out our things, we head for the picturesque old part of the town, both of us fairly limping along. Perhaps, I should speak for myself. Who do we run into but our friends from Paris. We sit and have wine together one last time in a bustling, chic little restaurant. We raise a toast to all of us and to the Camino. *"Buen Camino!"* They are continuing for a few more days until their holiday comes to an end. We are heading home to the States, weaving our way back to Paris tomorrow morning on the train. Parting is such a sweet sorrow with these fleeting friends of ours from the Camino. After we part ways, Marcia and I locate a restaurant nearby and order up plates of tasty crepes. Then we head home to our pilgrim retreat for much needed rest and sleep, glorious sleep.

Very early this morning, we walk back across a long bridge by the river and then a mile or two through town to *la gare* (the train station). We are fortunate to book two seats on the TGV (speed train) back to Paris. What a sweet adventure. Our old mentor Nancy Drew must have been smiling down on us from a distant twinkling star, cheering us on, as we walked the Camino. "*Vous allez!*" Yes, you go girls! As we bid the Camino *au revoir* once more, both of us staring out the windows of the train as the landscape speeds by, I lean back for a nap and imagine Nancy, yet again, whispering to us to return someday soon. "*À bientôt!*"

II.
Spring 2012
Figeac to Condom

164 MILES—13 DAYS

Figeac, Gréalou, Mas del Pech, Vaylats, Le Pech,
Ferme Trigodina, Lascabanes, Montlauzan,
Gîte Pigeonnaire, Moissac, Auvillar, Miradoux,
Lectoure, La Romieu, Condom

*Hear, I beseech thee, and I will speak: I will demand of thee,
and declare thou unto me. —Job 42:4*

Yes, I have wrangled with God like the biblical Job—although I can hardly compare myself with Job. Let's just say I recognize some of his struggles in my own. You know: willfulness, self-righteousness, confusion, self-pity, finally submission, and then recognition. I prefer not to wrangle with the Divine anymore, if I can help it. I am trying to figure out the signs and symbols in my life, so that I recognize and follow the waymarks—kind of like following those red and white lines painted on the sidewalks, and stone walls, and trees on the Camino. Sometimes I get it right. Sometimes I have to double back—such is my life.

On our first trip on the Camino, as we were heading back to Paris on the train from Figeac, the train made a brief stop at the station on the outskirts of Rocamadour. It was all I could do to contain myself. I wanted to leap off the train to explore that beautiful medieval village I had read so much about. Disappointed, I made a mental note to come back there *tout de suite*, which is now being realized. Marcia and I have flown into Paris once more and have taken the train south, the train stopping several times until we finally reach Rocamadour. We grab our backpacks and excitedly get off at the small station where we ask how to get to the old section of the town. "*Bonjour, Monsieur. Comment allez-vous? Où est la ville Rocamadour, s'il vous plait?*... so much for my French. Fortunately for us, a station employee, smiling kindly and with some amount of animation (since he knows we won't understand otherwise), points us to a footpath right behind the train station that will take us there. We thank him profusely. So now we are making our own mini pilgrimage, through wooded areas and down dirt roads by outlying houses, to Rocamadour. We walk over two miles.

Before leaving for France, we had booked two nights at Le Terminus des Pèlerins, a charming hotel that I had found on the internet. It is located in the ancient walled part of the village. As we enter Rocamadour, we pass by numerous shops, restaurants, and hotels situated on one side of a gouge by the Alzou River, what we read is a tributary of the Rive Dordogne in southwestern France. As we gaze over the deep divide, the medieval complex of cathedrals and chapels that is ancient Rocamadour looms high on the rocky cliffs on the other side—it is a spectacular sight to see. We look in some shops and find hiking poles. Unfortunately, we have had to buy hiking poles once more since they are now banned as carry-on items due to terrorist threats. Having purchased new poles, we then take a path through the valley over to the old walled city. We pass through the turreted entrance and walk the narrow cobblestone street lined with more shops. And there it is—our perfectly charming hotel. It sits right across the street from a long flight of stairs leading up to the cathedral complex. A most delightful shop is situated next door, its windows piled high with candied dried fruit au chocolat beneath a hot pink and white awning. It is a fanciful mix of old and new. Madame, the owner at our hotel, is gracious, and she speaks some English. We climb a flight of stairs to reach our small room, complete with two twin beds and a private bathroom. The windows overlook the busy cobblestone street below. We are almost eye to eye with the lower reaches of the cathedral, all a cozy welcome to our stay here. It is early evening by now, and we unpack a bit and go down to eat at the hotel restaurant. We order mushroom and cheese omelettes, salads, and le vin rouge in the lovely dining room painted a deep peach.

Later that evening, when we are nestled in our beds, I read that Rocamadour has been a sacred site for centuries, first celebrating the three goddesses associated with Cybele and then, in the Middle Ages, becoming a Marian shrine and pilgrimage destination. According to legend, the incorrupt body of a hermit, who loved God and practiced devotional solitude, was found here, and so came forth the name for the area, Roc-Amadour, the "rock of the lover." Pilgrims started to make the trek to visit and venerate a statue of the Blessed Virgin Mary found in a chapel built high into the recesses of the rocks. This dark wooden statue is thought to be the work of the hermit. Today the main cathedral, Notre Dame de Rocamadour, houses this Black Virgin. There is some speculation that the hermit, Amadour, was, in fact, Zacheus, from biblical times. It is believed that Zacheus traveled to this region after Jesus's death to escape persecution. A crypt and chapel dedicated to St. Amador now lie below the Cathedral—his relics and his legend, it seems, forever shrouded in time and mystery.

We awake early, excited to go out and explore the village. It is also our birthday. We are sixty-one years old today. Marcia opens her birthday card. A big yellow cat meows out the birthday jingle. "Meow, meow, meow, meow, meow, meow…" I guess it gets lost in the translation—silly us sometimes. We do like to laugh. We have petit déjeuner downstairs on the balcony overlooking the river gorge and then walk across the cobbled street to the stairs leading up to the cathedral. We have read that true penitents climb the long staircase on their knees. I have to say we pass on that, but make our way up slowly just the same. It is a beautiful clear day, and the bright blue sky dips down to greet us. As we climb, the turrets and walls of the Castle of Rocamadour come into full view. The château, standing at the top of the rocky outcropping, guards the cathedral and chapel complex just below it. As we walk the castle rampart in the cool breeze, we have an expansive view of the river valley—it is fairly dazzling. After purchasing tickets, we head for the cathedral to see the Black Madonna and Child. This Madonna is very small and sits high, mounted on the wall in the main part of the cathedral before a red and gold backdrop. Gold *fleurs-de-lis* on azure blue flank the bottom walls beside her. A second Black Madonna and Child stand behind a small wooden boat in a side chamber. Here, she is portrayed as the patron saint of ships and sailors who seek her protection on the high seas. Blue and red votive candles glow softly at her feet. We look around some more. Life-size carvings of angels are suspended on the walls at the back of the cathedral. We snap pictures for awhile and rest and pray and try to absorb its beauty.

By nightfall, the cathedral and chapel complex are lit up in gold and green. Even the staircase is aglow. We walk this cobblestone street one last time to a restaurant nearby for dinner. We can now humbly add our names to the long list of pilgrims on the Santiago de Compostela pilgrimage who tarried for a time in Rocamadour before pressing west once more.

Prayers laid at the foot of the cross just outside Figeac

By morning, our gracious host has arranged a taxi to take us to the train station for our trip to Figeac, where we are resuming the Camino. We are fortunate once again to book seats on the train without reservations. Disembarking in Figeac, we make our way to the Camino to follow the waymarks once more. We will be on the GR 65 for a little over thirteen miles before reaching Gréalou, where we hope to find a gîte d' étape for the night. We have already walked two or three miles, at least, through Figeac. We figure sixteen miles is enough for our first day back on the Camino. Just outside Figeac, we reach a large stone cross. Notes and prayers are tucked under a mound of stones at its base. I have carried prayers from some of my friends back home, as well as my own personal note to God, which I place here at the first cross we see on the Camino. The backdrop of lush green meadows, aqua sky, and luminous clouds invites us to stop for awhile and take a picture. We stop again and visit a lovely church in the village of Faycelles. Leaving the village of Faycelles, we are walking through woods on a shady dirt path.

As we reach the Hamlet of Mas de la Croix, our walking guide gives us a choice of routes: through the Vallée de Célé or on the old Roman road on a limestone plateau called the Cami Ferrat. We choose the Roman route, not wanting to miss out on anything historical. When we reach Gréalou, we visit the beautiful Romanesque church of Notre Dame of the Assumption. We then find space nearby at the modern gîte at Ecoasis owned and run by a young couple. At dinner we are served plates piled high with steaming lasagna and green olives, salads, sumptuous brownies au chocolat, and finally raspberry *glace*. There is good humor, chatter in several languages, and excitement around the long crowded table. By evening, the *gîte* is booked full. Later, we slip quietly into our bunks for the night, both of us fairly exhausted. I carefully pull off the band-aid on one of my feet to let a blister dry out. Supposedly, you must then puncture the blister with a needle and pull thread through it to drain it. *Pas merci, pas moi!* Noooo thank you—not me! I'll take my chances without it.

This morning, we enjoy our slices of toasted baguettes, jam, and cafe au lait and leave early. We are anxious to get through the Cami Ferrat. We heed the warning to stock up on food and water for this section of the Camino—clue number one. We have packed up sliced baguette ham sandwiches for lunch and dried fruit and nuts for snacks.

We reach an old dolmen which is pictured in our book and snap our own photo of it. A dolmen, we read, is an ancient megalithic tomb with upright stones forming a base which supports a large flat capstone. There it is on our path: Exhibit A. There are supposed to be many in this area.

I figure I better look up the English translation for the word "*cause.*" Perhaps, had I done it sooner, we would have taken the variant route along the River Célé. But, oh no, we have opted for the Roman historic route. I see it means "limestone desert." Another definition I find is "wilds." Take your pick. We are trudging up a steep, slippery, rocky, narrow path on the causeway. It seems to go on forever. *Un taxi, s'il vous plait!*

Just kidding, Dear God! And, as it begins to rain, the temperature drops significantly, and Marcia starts to get numbness in her fingers. Mind you, this is *with* gloves on. She is trying to stay calm. "Don't worry, Marcia!" I exclaim. But that's like throwing flames on the fire. "What if it's something serious?" she moans. It reminds me of one time when Marcia and I were hiking in the woods when we were young girls. Our dog Sandy, a beagle, suddenly ran off, barking wildly. We thought she was dying. She eventually returned unharmed. When we got home and told the tale, Mother laughed and laughed and explained that Sandy had caught the scent of a rabbit. Well, now I am hoping it is only a

Painted from Peter Paul Rubens' the Immaculate Conception

rabbit again—if you get my point. It is a loose association, I realize.

We finally reach an open carport by an abandoned house and take shelter from the downpour for a while and eat our picnic lunch. The cold rain is pinging on the roof. Thunder pounds nearby. Neither of us feels too good about sitting much longer under a metal roof. We can go back or go forward. Isn't that just another metaphor for life! We continue up the steep trail and eventually reach civilization and a gîte at Mas del Pech. Wet and bedraggled are we. The rain has stopped by now, and the sun, which is beginning to set, is peeking out of the clouds. Speaking of dogs, a sweet pregnant dog, wagging her tail and grinning ear to ear, comes out to greet us at the gîte. "A watchdog on pregnancy leave," I joke. Marcia manages a smile, but just barely.

This gîte is a beautiful old stone farmhouse with a red tile roof. Ivy winds up the pointed tower by the house. Purple iris and white sweet alyssum line the steps by the porch. Thankfully, there is space for us. Marcia decides she was either developing hypothermia from the cold rain, or she had some sort of temporary pinched nerve in her shoulder from lugging her backpack. I would add a little hysteria to the diagnosis. With rest that night, she recuperates.

We are hoping to reach the Monastère des Filles de Jésus in Vaylats by early evening. We will walk almost eighteen miles today, but the terrain is somewhat flat. We wind mostly up dirt roads through woods and fields. We are still on the Cami Ferrat (the path of iron), but it seems kinder to us today. We have read that the monastery takes pilgrims. At this point, Marcia is walking up quickly along a narrow wooded path. I am following just behind her trying to keep up. She suddenly stops. The desperate shrill of a bird is piercing the air. Turning around to me, she whispers, "Did you hear *that*? Let's stop." And, just as she turns back around, she freezes, as a large snake slithers across the path at her feet and then into the dense underbrush. Yes, Marcia almost became the modern Mary trampling the serpent! "It's a snake!" OMG—now, it's my turn for hysterics. By God's grace, I only get to see the last gentle rustle of the leaves as the snake slides into the woods again. Serpent or snake, get me out of here! It is all I can do to force myself up the trail. I am running like my pants are on fire—hysterical me. Mother always said, "Where there's one, there are others." Did I say that these old words of wisdom aren't helping me very much right about now? *Calm down, you silly girl. Just calm down*, I say to myself. This is easier said than done, as I am beating a path out of there. Let's just say, I have a better appreciation for Marcia's fear of birds. Yes indeed! So, did the bird warn *us*, or did it warn the *snake*, or both?

The Monastère des Filles de Jésus is a huge, beautiful old concrete and stone château with tall white iron gates at the entrance. We walk through the open gate praying we will find room here. We have read we *must* call ahead, but, of course, we have not done so. A lay volunteer is posted at an office at the front entrance checking pilgrims in, including, as it turns out, *us*. To say we are grateful and relieved would be an under statement. We are directed to a small private room like a monastic cell. We also have a private bathroom. The nuns, who run the gîte, are very dear. We are served dinner here, cafeteria style, in a large dining room in the basement. The pilgrims sit at one long table, the nuns, most of them elderly, at another. They say prayers and clap and cheer us on as we take turns announcing our countries of origin. The fact that we are all together and that they are allowing us a glimpse into their personal world is a precious thing. Most of these nuns are retired and are living out their days here in this faith community. After dinner, we attend a vespers service with them which includes a pilgrim blessing.

Walking West on the Camino—Encore Une Fois

The Pont Valentre over the Lot River leaving Cahors

By morning, one of the nuns is busy out back, feeding several semi-feral cats at her feet. It is a sweet thing to see. St. Francis would be proud. After petit déjeuner and as we are leaving, Marcia and I pose for a photo at a mound of rocks that have been stacked up below a small stone figure of a monk. We then continue on a dirt path through the woods, on the Camino once more. We are not too sure how long we will walk today or where we will stay—until we happen upon the Gîte Saint-Antoine near the hamlets of Flaujac-Poujois and Le Pech. We have walked almost fifteen miles. Mme. Therese, who lives in a large house next door, owns and runs the gîte. She is most welcoming to us. We get the impression she has not formally opened yet, since it is early spring, but she kindly accommodates us anyway. She calls up her sister, who immediately rushes over, and they begin to prepare our meal. We communicate as best we can back and forth with our bad French and their bad English. We learn our gracious host herself walked the Camino several times with her husband, who is now deceased. Big hearts rule the day here. They leave us to enjoy our dinner of fresh pasta and chicken and green salads. They are charmed we are twins. We are charmed they are so kind and so generous, *tous les deux*—both of them.

We backtrack slightly the next morning down the Chemin de Saint Jacques to get back on the Camino. We are headed for Cahors, almost eight miles away. As we cross a bridge over the Lot River, we are greeted at Accueil Pèlerins, a small pilgrim welcome center. Volunteers are serving tea and biscuits and kindly answering questions about the Camino, as well as about their town. We spend a large part of the day in Cahors walking the cobblestone streets and visiting the cathedrals and churches in the old section. It is a large town, a lovely blend of modern and medieval. But what I find most fascinating is the grand old

Pont Valentré, which we cross as we leave Cahors. We look for a devil that supposedly is carved high on the second tower of the bridge. The story goes that the master mason made a pact with the devil to complete the work of the bridge but then double-crossed the old devil in the end. The devil had the last laugh, however. That devil smiles gleefully down on us still as we pass under him, making our way across the bridge. I turn around to catch a second glimpse, but he has vanished, that ole devil.

We take the variant route to the right as we leave the bridge and eventually reach the Croix de Magne, a large cross overlooking the town. The other choice leaving the bridge was to go left and then up a steep hill, the main route on the GR 65. We think we have added at least two miles to our walk in going around the hill. Big lesson here: often, taking the direct yet more difficult path is easier in the long run. This is another instance in which we see our efforts to choose less has created more—by that I mean more miles, more angst. Beware of shortcuts. But how would we know, in this moment or in life in general? I am just saying.

We walk on and on and on looking for the tiny village of L'Hospitale, hoping we will find a gîte for the night there. We never find it, and now we are walking in dense woods and down narrow dirt roads in the middle of nowhere. I write in my journal that we walked eleven hours this day. Eventually, half-dead, we reach a gîte at Ferme Trigodina. It is eight o'clock in the evening, and as we stumble along and finally emerge from the underbrush, there it is, like a mirage. There are beds for us, but our host has to scramble to find us something to eat. Other fellow pilgrims have already eaten and are heading for bed. I don't know. Are we fortunate or unfortunate this day on the Camino? I say we are fortunate, but you decide.

The next day, we reach the village of Lascabanes. We have walked only eight miles, but after our rather grueling excursion yesterday, we are not counting the miles. Our walking guide says we will find a *gîte* here attached to the church. We locate it fairly easily. However, it is full, per Cecilia, who is in charge of the lodging. We sit outside for awhile wondering what to do. We have already fairly begged her saying that we would be fine with sleeping on the floor. *Ce n'est pas de problème!* We just want shelter for the night at this point. Shortly, Cecilia runs out excitedly and tells us she has made room for us—bless that girl. Two bunk beds. Dare I say it, it feels like a miracle.

In early evening we walk next door to the church attached to the gîte and attend a special pilgrim mass. The local priest, in his humble way, washes each pilgrim's feet, ours included. It is clearly a heart-level practice for him. The apse at the front displays strikingly beautiful statues of Jesus, St. Michael, and saints all around. A lovely old chandelier hanging just above us sparkles in the candlelight.

Later, at dinner, we sit with a lively group of German folk singers who are also walking the Camino. Some of the men are up singing and dancing around the long table, drinking too much, and generally toasting the moment. Marcia enjoys it. I find it to be a bit too much, but they are gracious indeed to include us in their festivities. I am struck by a painting that hangs above the piano in the dining room; it depicts a young peasant girl in the fields surrounded in dense mist. It is hauntingly beautiful. Our sweet host serves up some of the best pilgrim fare we have had yet: pureed vegetable soup, tasty vinegar chicken, fresh green beans, steamy mounds of mashed potatoes, and large helpings of apple crunch for dessert. Afterward, we drag ourselves up to bed. I am almost too tired to sleep. Morning comes quickly just the same.

Chapel Glow

We are refreshed and out early the next morning walking through rolling hills and vineyards. We visit a beautiful little church near Montcug, almost five miles along the Camino. In it, we surprisingly find another Black Madonna and Child to the right of the nave. She, who is small and dark, is mounted on the wall, bathed in the soft glow of candlelight. An image of the crucified Christ is on the left. The sun casts dancing diffused rays of light through the stained glass windows in a small interior chamber behind the altar. My painting hardly does it justice, it is so lovely.

We have read that this area is part of the Languedoc in southern France, where the Merovingian kings and the Cathars waged their wars. As I research the rich history of the region, the philosophic and religious wars seem to rage on to this day, yet all the more surrounded in mystery and intrigue. The Cathars (also known as the Abiginsians) practiced a form of gnostic dualism which brought them into direct conflict with the Roman Catholic Church, who branded them heretics. In dualism, the Godhead is comprised of a benevolent deity in the heavenly realms and his less powerful opposite, Lucifer or Satan, who rules the physical world. "Gnosis" means spiritual knowledge. The Cathars were apparently immensely popular among the common people and thus greatly threatened the power and wealth of the Church.

I also read that early Christian Gnostics did not venerate the cross but focused on the resurrection of Jesus and the light of the Holy Spirit in the world, as well as the teachings of Jesus per se. The great Chartres Cathedral near Paris contains no images of Jesus on the cross—the reach of Cathartic influence was rather far, it seems. The so-called "cult of Mary Magdalene" originated in the Languedoc region, especially around Rennes-le-Château, which is southeast of the Camino in southern France. Mary Magdalene, whom, it is written, Jesus loved the most, was thought by some to be one of his disciples. Further, it is claimed that the Merovingian kings descended directly from the holy bloodline of Jesus and Mary Magdalene, thus associating them with conspiracy theories even to this day. Some believe that the first Merovingian king initiated the crusades to the Holy Land, not only to fight the Moors, but also to recapture the esoteric secrets and wealth of the Temple of Solomon. The Knights Templars formed the protective arm of the Merovingian dynasty traveling back and forth from Jerusalem. Then, on one Friday the thirteenth, in 1307, the powerful French Templars were decimated and their power and reach of influence destroyed. It is thought that they went underground, founding secret societies that still flourish today. I realize I may be digressing and perhaps have wandered off the Camino.

Black Madonnas are common in French cathedrals, many of these cathedrals originally funded and built by the Knights Templar and their kings. Some say that the Black Virgins are a holdover from early pagan goddess worship, later transmuted into the "cult of the Virgin Mary" by the Catholic Church. What I do know personally is that I love the paintings and images of the Blessed Mary that abound in the churches on the Way. For me, they are, among other things, a symbol of the feminine aspect of the Divine. And why shouldn't there be a feminine aspect to God? Over half of this world is female. Perhaps God shines forth as spirit with no designation as masculine or feminine at all. And yes, I am aware of the biblical admonition that the female derived from Adam's rib. Okay, I will stop now—having most likely stirred up a hornet's nest along the Way. *Oh la la*—run girl run!

By the time we near Montlauzan, we have come almost ten miles. A green topiary in the form of a cross stands to the left, and we turn right heading into Montlauzan. Just before the village, we come upon a private gîte in an old stone presbytery which we discover is owned and run by a friendly British couple. The gîte is booked solid for the evening now that we have snapped up the last two beds. The owners point out an image etched high on an exposed old wall in the living room. It is the Oculus Dei, the all-seeing eye of God, within a triangle—the triangle or pyramid symbolizing the Holy Trinity. This ancient symbol spans various cultures and traditions, including early Gnostic thought and later, Freemasonry and sacred geometry. I find it fascinating to see it here. Our hosts prepare the pilgrim meal for a full house. We eat and are all in bed early. I ate so quickly and ran so fast for my bed that I can hardly tell you what I ate, except that it was delicious and thoughtfully prepared.

It takes us quite a while to get through the large town of Lauzerte this morning. We have stopped here for lunch at a small restaurant. Marcia snaps a picture of our pilgrim fare: French omelettes, green salads, and buttery baguette toasts all piled high on our plates. It is worthy of a picture. After lunch, we carry on and pass a large white dovecote near the village of Le Chartron. We snap pictures again. We see that dovecotes (which house pigeons) are common in this area. It is starting to rain. We find shelter at another magnificently beautiful Romanesque church, the Église Saint-Serin du Bosc.

This is also an area of an intensely beautiful expanse of yellow flowers which we learn later are used to make canola oil. We reach an area where we hear rather alarming unrecognizable, intense, loud sounds. We find ourselves in *froggyville*—a veritable marshy green bog of hundreds of frogs out serenading the pilgrims along the Camino. Next, we pass down dirt roads and walk through vineyards and fields of red poppies and wildflowers as we wind our way through the picturesque countryside. We eventually reach Gîte Pigeonnier where we spend the night— thirteen miles this day. For roughly forty dollars, we have booked bunk beds, dinner, and petit déjeuner, that we have learned now is called a *"demi-pension."* For dinner, we are served vegetable soup, then duck and potatoes and salad, and finally a custard for

On the Camino au Printemps

dessert. Marcia is quite jubilant not to have run into any pigeons. This day feels like one of our most difficult because, towards the end, a lot of the Camino wound steadily uphill, almost endlessly.

It is ten miles to the large town of Moissac, our goal for today's walk. It takes us quite a while to reach the old section of town where we are anxious to find the Abbaye Saint-Pierre. This Abbey, another UNESCO World Heritage Site, was once a Benedictine monastery, dating back to the seventh century. But first, upon asking about gîtes in the area in our limited French, we are directed to the Gîte Ultreïa located near the train station and owned by a young Irish couple. *Ultreïa* means loosely "ever onward." It is located right on the Camino and down from the abbey church. We are glad to get beds in this friendly refuge. We unpack and regroup and then head out to buy tomorrow's picnic lunch and more cat food. We also peruse some trendy little shops nearby and then make it to the church just in time for six o'clock vespers. We are glad not to miss it, for the nuns chant beautifully in the nave.

The Abbey Church of Saint Pierre and its cloisters contain some of the finest Romanesque art in France. Most noteworthy are the tympanum, as you enter the church, which depicts scenes from the Book of Revelation, and a statue of Jeremiah, the Prophet. Many of the stone carvings are rather grotesque, I suppose typical of early medieval themes warning against the dangers of hell and unbridled sexuality. There is a notably dark statue of Saint Jacques inside the church, as well as a magnificent old painting of The Last Supper. Mary Magdalene, whom Leonardo da Vinci famously placed to the right of Jesus in his painting of The Last Supper, is noticeably missing from this painting. Tonight, our dinner is served on long picnic tables outside in the back courtyard. Once again, the gîte is full.

This morning, we have our customary petit déjeuner of toasted baguettes, café au lait, and fresh orange juice. The air is full of laughter and good cheer. We meet a retired couple from Australia who are walking the Way from Le Puy to Santiago—almost a thousand miles. He has constructed a type of sled he hopes will carry their backpacks across the Pyrenees. It makes me wonder just how I am going to get *myself* across those mountains, much less my backpack.

Leaving the gîte, we walk to the left of a canal along a towpath. Fortunately, it is flat and shaded by tall poplars, but as the morning progresses, the heat intensifies. There is no shade anywhere. We stop and rest frequently and splash our faces with water. Marcia and I suffered heat exhaustion a few years ago while visiting a seaside resort in Mexico, an experience neither of us wants to repeat. It scared us both. Nevertheless, we have set our sights on the medieval village of Auvillar twelve miles from Moissac. We are now entering the region of the Midi-Pyrénées. As we approach Auvillar, we have a splendid view of the town atop a hill by the Rive Garonne. Auvillar is another one of *les plus beaux villages de France*. It is easy to see why. As we enter the Place de la Halle (the town square), we are met by a large, delicate iron cross towering over the cobblestone streets. Nearby stands a restored old circular market and arcade with white pillars, that I learn later was once a corn exchange. Lovely little shops and flower markets line the narrow streets.

As we first entered the village, we noticed a charming hotel and restaurant, Gîte Le Petit Baladin, its brick walls covered in ivy. We double back and inquire within about beds for the night. We are pleased to learn it has rooms for pilgrims, and we wind our way up a circular staircase to a private room on the top floor. We have been given two single white iron beds, back to back, in a long narrow small room overlooking the interior gardens. The red curtains flap in the breeze at the open window. The shutters creak. This is as sweet a spot as we have found anywhere. But it is a quirky hotel to be sure—a parlor table, a chair, and a piano have been bolted upside down to the ceiling in the bar area. This adds a strange ambiance indeed. It is, to me, reminiscent of the old TV show, "The Munsters."

Marcia and I unpack and go back downstairs to sit outside and enjoy coconut ice cream cones served up by our friendly host and his wife. We then head for the twelfth-century parish Church of Saint-Pierre. It is just off the main square. A modern little wooden pilgrim, placed high on the corner of an old brick building, seems to greet us on our way to the church. A beautiful old stone cathedral it is, with its sublime rose window, stained glass, and sparkling crystal chandelier. Another statue of St. James, the pilgrim, stands in the interior of the church amid long white tapered candles glowing in the semi-darkness. Flowers have been placed at his feet.

At dinner back at the hotel, we are surprised to find our new Aussi friends seated at a table outside the restaurant. They are staying here too. We join them and all order the specially priced pilgrim meal: mounds of spicy chicken curry and rice, green salads, egg custard, and le vin rouge. *Bon appétit!* Despite our sore feet, we are charmed by this day once again. And, as darkness descends on Auvillar, we are already tucked in our beds plotting our route for tomorrow. My legs and feet are aching, but I am hoping by morning that they will be ready to carry on. Ready or not—*ultreïa!*

As we leave Auvillar, we pass under an old clock tower on our way out of the village. A hamlet just past Auvillar invites us to turn left down a lane of overhanging pollarded trees, but it is off the Camino, and we keep straight ahead. I was so curious about these strange looking cropped trees, so common to southern France, that I had to research them. And yes, every year or two, the branches of plane trees are chopped off to create a knobby sculpture-like appearance, so odd looking, but beautiful too.

Almost five miles into today's journey, we reach the medieval village of Saint-Antoine. The village is dominated by a château which was once a hospital set up to treat people with Ergotism, also known as St. Anthony's Fire. This condition resulted from eating infected rye bread, which caused gangrene to hands and feet. I shudder to think of what misery it must have caused in the darkness of the Middle Ages. The hospital is a beautiful turreted stone castle now, half-covered in ivy, sitting behind a tall, brown wrought iron fence. The village, as we pass through, is quaint and lovely, comprised of one main street around the old church. Inside the church, we find a statue of St. Anthony surrounded in azure, as well as a colorful statue of St. George slaying a dragon. This church is exquisite with its peach-and-green vaulted ceiling and dark apricot rosettes painted on the walls. It is time to press on, but we are reluctant to leave.

Almost three miles later, we come to the village of Flamarens, where we find a twelfth-century castle in the middle of repairs. Marcia and I want to rest and drink water and eat apples at a picnic table nearby. No sooner have we sat down than up leaps a large, friendly gray cat who is only too pleased to sit and purr in my lap. Next appears an elderly gentleman who joins us at the table. His English is good. He tells us that this ball of fur in my lap named "Mew" once belonged to a neighbor. His neighbor's wish was to "put down" his cat when he died. Wish not granted! He also explains that he had been a school teacher in the village for many years, and that later, he and his wife had traveled extensively. Now, as they are aging, they have taken up the cause of caring for and feeding the stray cats, as well as dogs, in the village. Out of compassion, they *see* where others never even notice or look up. My take—there are a lot of hungry cats along the Camino whom most people, I guess, believe can fend

Iron cross on bridge near Auvillar

for themselves catching mice and birds. We have met a kindred spirit in this kind and gentle man.

We are headed next for Miradoux, which is almost three miles away. We hope to secure beds for the night there. Miradoux is a considerably larger village, but we find the gîtes and hotels booked up. We keep hearing about a new gîte called Bonté Divine which may have beds. Of course, Marcia noticed their sign as we entered the village, but I had wanted to continue on down the main street—a big mistake. Now we have to double back, our feet complaining all the way. This is a beautiful new modern gîte with an inner courtyard and, most importantly, a *demi-pension* for us. Our host's wife, as it turns out, is a designer, who has painted her version of the Assumption of the Blessed Mary. It hangs on the wall as you enter. It is beautiful and wistful, this Mary, surrounded in a vortex of silvery clouds and dark mist. After unpacking, we visit the Gothic church at Miradoux, which is close by. In it are gorgeous paintings of Jesus and Mary and a wooden carving of St. James. The sun casts rays of golden light through the stained glass windows—angel dust, no doubt.

Early the next morning as we carry on, Marcia and I visit another Gothic church in Castet-Arrouy. Inside the church, we find a lovely statue of Saint Germaine. She wears a pink and green simple frock and a white apron. Little Germaine is a peasant girl, a bouquet of flowers in one hand, a loaf of bread in the other, a lamb at her feet. Later, I look up information on St. Germaine. It seems that Germaine Cousin was born in 1579 in Pibrac, a remote village in France about ten miles from Toulouse. She was unwanted and so was cast out into the barn, a dirty shepherd girl with no shoes and a withered arm. Nevertheless, Germaine was devoted to the Rosary and to loving God. She died at age twenty-two. Many years later, when her body was interred, it was found to be uncorrupted and strangely beautiful. She is said to be the patron saint of abused and neglected children.

Joan of Arc

This is one of the most beautiful churches we have visited, this Church of Saint-Blandine, with its vaulted ceiling painted mint green and gold. Jesus, and Mary, and angels gaze down on us from above. White wildflowers, twinkling stars, and *fleurs-de-lis* surround them all about. You just have to look up. But isn't that always the way it is?

By evening, we are hoping to stay in a convent in Lectoure, but it is full. We have come twelve more miles. Lectoure is a large town in the Gers, in Gascony, a region in southern France. It takes us quite a while to get through the town. Happily, we find a pleasant gîte with Madame Veronica and secure bunk beds and a pilgrim meal. It is nice to feel secure after all. But, of course, there are more hungry cats around, which we feed.

As we head out this morning, I am looking forward to seeing the old Chapelle de'Abrin, a former outpost for the Knights Hospitallers of St. John of Jerusalem, but it eludes us. A lot eludes us this day. We must have missed a waymark somewhere, happily chatting as we passed it by unawares. We find ourselves now wandering around lost, but apparently not lost to the Divine. We end up taking a paved but narrow rural road directly to La Romieu, what we learn later was probably a shortcut just off the Camino. I like shortcuts especially if they are, let's say, by divine appointment. Lost and then found!

La Romieu, as it turns out, is a beautiful, quaint little village with an interesting history about cats. A booklet from the tourist office next to the cathedral reads: *"Visitez la cité des chats."* They aren't kidding—this place of the cats! More about that later. In the early fourteenth century, Pope Clement V took an interest in this refuge on the Camino and built the large collegiate church and cloister here, now a UNESCO World Heritage Site. We are anxious to visit it, but more anxious to find accommodations for the night. *Mademoiselle*, at a café nearby, points us back up the narrow cobbled street to our identified gîte, but we continue to wander around until we finally locate it, our refuge in plain sight. Having been renovated, it is a large gîte at the former La Convent de la Romieu. Rows of luscious pink rosebushes line the sidewalks to the entrance. I don't know how we missed it. Our host leads us up massive stone stairs to the second floor and a large dormitory room of bunk beds. For about twenty-five dollars, we have booked beds and petit déjeuner for the next morning.

And now, it is out to visit La Romieu and its collegiate church. The church itself is most beautiful with its stained glass windows shining prisms of bright colored light into the nave. We find a lovely statue of Joan of Arc, dressed in a long, flowing agua skirt. Her silver sword held high, she is leading the cry to battle. Gregorian chant fills the smoky candle-perfumed air. Marcia and I climb the steep and precarious spiral stone stairs to the top of the tower for a beautiful view of the surrounding area. I wonder what it must have been like as a monk to pad softly up those stairs by candlelight and to ring the bells—their mournful toll echoing across the valley mixing with the howl of the cold winds.

Back down again, we explore the extensive, lovely gardens beside the church and then walk over to the village square. We are delighted to see life-size cats in stone crouched on window sills and peeking around corners—it is all so curious. It seems that, about the mid-fourteenth century, a little girl named Angeline saved the village from an outbreak of the plague—her cats decimated the mouse population. In fact, a bust of the child is mounted in the town square, pointy ears and all. So goes the tail, I mean tale, of the lovely little village of La Romieu.

We cross the square and dine outside on omelettes and salads for an early supper. As we sip red wine, the sun begins to set in the clear blue sky. We are reflecting on our journey this year and, especially, on how fortunate we are to walk through these French villages, one by one, each unique, with its own story to tell. La Romieu is the icing on the cake. And, as a blazing orange sunset approaches, we head home for a long catnap, smiling all the way—we, the *catgirls*.

Today, we hope to reach Condom, our last stop on the Camino for this year before we go back to the States. About four miles down shady lanes and then through grassy fields, after crossing the Rive Auvignon, we reach the Chapelle Saint Germaine. This old stone chapel was once a monastery, laid waste by the Normans in the ninth century. Rebuilt, it was dedicated to St. Germaine. Inside, we discover another beautiful statue of St. Germaine, as well as one of St. Jacques. Multi-colored diffused sunlight pours through the magnificent stained glass windows and floods the sanctuary. The tapered candles, all aglow at the altar, have invited the light in, it seems, for a brief dance. And then, as quickly as it came, it is gone—the dance card played.

Outside again, we have befriended a kitty at a picnic table nearby. Our backpacks and hiking poles are already flung down in the grass. It is time to go home to reality, or is *this* reality? It is certainly our reality this day, and we savor the moment for a long while, both of us now stretched out in the grass under the shade of the tall trees by the chapel. "I think I'll take a snooze," I tell Marcia. "Yeah, you wish," she laughs, for we have more miles to go. Reluctantly, we leave this peaceful place and carry on.

Condom is a large bustling Gascon town known for its Armagnac brandy. We are anxious to get there. After some amount of searching, we finally locate the Gîte L'Ancien Carmel de Condom down Avenue Victor Hugo. This large old Carmelite monastery, now refurbished, offers rooms for pèlerins. *"Oui, Madames, une chambre pour vous!"* Thank God! And, I do mean that literally, because we are both rather exhausted. After unpacking and doing our usual drill, we drag ourselves back out into the street to explore the town and to check out the local street fair. We are excited to find a small British market and to have an actual conversation with the proprietor as we purchase our supplies for the next day. And then, delighted still, we run into our Australian friends on the street. Snapping more pictures of everyone, we hug and say goodbye for the last time. *"Buen Camino, mes amis! Bon Chemin!"* As we go home, they go on.

Thoughts go round and round in my head as I am drifting off to sleep this night. What makes a good Camino? Is it the friends we meet? Is it the sublime old churches and their art? Is it that we don't fall down and break an arm or sprain an ankle? Or is it that I *do* and yet walk on? Is it that we find beds every night like clockwork? Is it the mud and rocky trails we stumble through? Or, that grassy winding path lined with red poppies and wildflowers? Is it those cows and mules who seem to greet us as we pass them by along the Way? My feet are aching as I sink deeper into my little bed just as swirls of golden candlelight sweep in to lift me off to my dreams. But not before I think of those old words of wisdom again and "call it all good" after all.

Leaving the Camino this morning, we are heading north for the port city of Bordeaux, another UNESCO World Heritage Site. We are traveling there via Agen by bus and then taking a train to Bordeaux. Negotiating trains and buses speaking little French can be a challenge, but, so far, we haven't headed off in the wrong direction. And maybe it wouldn't be so bad anyway, since Toulouse is just to the south. I would love to see it too. But that's for another trip. It is comforting for both of us to ride the bus at this point. We alight in Bordeaux and find a hotel nearby, the Etap.

This afternoon, we walk down by the Rive Garonne to explore Bordeaux and, especially, the Gothic Basilique Saint Michel. The Basilica's dark gray spires reach to the clouds—she has beckoned us to visit her. Inside, we see St. Michel slaying the dragon, glorious art portraying Jesus, and a statue of Mary with gold and dark green on the backdrop glittering around her. Starting in the fourteenth century, this church was constructed over a period of two hundred years. *C'est magnifique—cette église!*

Lovely old Bordeaux—with its silver castles and towers, narrow cobblestone streets, and colorful shops of all sorts. Tables and chairs under bright red umbrellas are set outside the restaurants in the square. People have gathered after work to toast the early evening and to sample their beautiful Bordeaux wines. It is a busy celebration of life, and friends, and very good wine. We pause for more pictures and then join them for our own celebration of sorts. *Bonsoir—À votre santé!*

By early morning, we are pestering the Frenchman behind the counter at the train station. *"Quelle ville est-ce que vous recommandez pour nous?"* I manage, as if he should know where we would like to visit next. We are looking for a destination on the train route back up to Paris. He picks out Tours for us, and we obediently oblige him and buy train tickets. Well, if you know a better way, let me know. Tours, we see, is in the Loire Valley just southwest of Paris. Luckily, the tourist office in Tours is just across the street from the train station. We walk over.

This is the region of gorgeously interesting castles, those same abodes of royalty that so starkly contrasted the rich and the poor and helped to fuel the French Revolution. We pick out the Renaissance Châteaux Villandry and Azay le Rideau and arrange to go on a small bus tour for the day. We also locate the Mercure Hotel within walking distance, where we book for two nights. Heading toward the castles later, I think how even royalty walked the Camino. Apparently, there are few class distinctions when you are attempting to redeem your soul—death being the great leveler. The rain does little to dampen our spirits at these two splendid *châteaux*, although we forego a walk around the famous manicured gardens at Villandry. The thought of wearing soggy hiking boots for the rest of the day is not appealing to either of us.

The city of Tours is quite interesting, separate and apart from the fact that it is a staging area for excursions to the castles nearby in the Loire Valley. We make it a point to see Saint Gatien's Cathedral. An exquisite mix of Romanesque, Gothic, and Renaissance architectural style, its construction began in 1170 after the earlier church was destroyed by fire in the sixth century. Behind the Cathedral stands the eighteenth-century archbishop's palace, now the magnificent Musée des Beaux-Arts de Tours. We spend a couple of hours here admiring the priceless masterpieces, including works by Rembrandt and Rubens. Finally, we walk the old section of Tours back to our hotel in the cool dusk of evening, just before turning in for the night.

We have managed to book a very early train to Paris this morning. And, once in Paris, yes, I have dragged Marcia back to Notre-Dame. I insist we go there despite the long lines and heat. We are inside sooner than we expect. Notre Dame is a magnet for me. I guess it is those gloriously mystical rose windows that are so transfixing. Interestingly, today there is also a lovely display in pictures and art of the life of Saint Teresa of Avila. Our Carmelite friends back home will enjoy my photos.

Back outside, we walk down the busy sidewalks and cross one of the long bridges over the River Seine into the Latin Quarter on the Left Bank, with its shops and cafés and flower markets. We stop in the Church of Saint Severin and then stroll past the Place Saint-Germain-des-Prés. We also walk to the Luxembourg Palace and its beautiful gardens and eventually get the Metro to the Airport Hilton for our last night in Paris. Don't forget—we have carried our backpacks all day long, and we have an early flight back to the States tomorrow morning. Tired are we and ready for bed.

This morning, as we walk from the Hilton to the airport terminal just across the street, we both look back at the skyline one last time. *Ah belle Paris—au revoir!*

III.
Spring 2013
Condom to Saint-Jean-Pied-de-Port

152 MILES—15 DAYS

Condom, Montréal-du-Gers, Eauze, Nogaro, Barcelonne-du-Gers, Miramont-Sensacq, Arzaco-Arraziguet, Uzan, Église d'Argagnon, Navarrenx, Lichos, Uhart-Mixe, Larceveau, Saint-Jean-Pied-de-Port

As the hart panteth after the water brooks,
so panteth my soul after thee, O God. —Psalms 42: 1

Now, in the spring of a new year, as I am preparing to start the next segment of the Camino, I retrieve my backpack from the closet—same bag as on the previous trips, but now smarter and lighter. We are Camino packers par excellence. Thirteen pounds max, including bottled water, picnic lunch, snacks, and cat food. I recommend you make plastic re-sealable baggies your best friends.

Here are the essentials:

- ☐ backpack (in Europe, called a rucksack) the lightest one you can find—no frills; a hip belt is a must as are padded shoulder straps. My backpack weighs less than a pound.
- ☐ sandals (for evening strolls around the village or from table to bunk bed)
- ☐ extra pair of underwear
- ☐ broad brimmed hiking hat (packable)
- ☐ plastic rain cape which covers body and backpack
- ☐ gloves
- ☐ one extra pair of hiking socks
- ☐ one extra blouse and pair of pants for after hiking (rolled up in a one-gallon baggie)
- ☐ one extra jacket stuffed in its own little bag (layer, layer, layer)
- ☐ silk sleeping bag shell, or any sleeping bag liner (yes, that's right—no sleeping bag)
- ☐ travel shampoo and conditioner, soap, shower cap, packets of laundry detergent
- ☐ small travel towel
- ☐ blister supplies, tweezers, nail clippers, travel blunt-end scissors, sunscreen, tissues
- ☐ walking guidebook
- ☐ camera
- ☐ flashlight
- ☐ hiking poles

- [ ] power bars and vitamin C/mineral packets (packed in a one-pint baggie)
- [ ] mascara, lipstick, lip balm, powder, blush (packed in a one-pint baggie)

No heavy *Miam Miam Dodo* book of maps and gîtes should be brought along (a very helpful book actually), unless you have torn out the pages and discarded them as you complete that part of the journey. And, Marcia has finally let go of her hair dryer. Both of us are still holding onto our mascara. I wonder if I will be still clutching my mascara and blush as I cross the veil someday. Wear good hiking boots and socks, hiking pants, a blouse or shirt, and a fleece or other lightweight jacket for early morning, depending on the weather and time of year. *Voilà!*

Marcia and I are returning to Condom to resume the Camino via side trips—first to Chartres and then to the Château de Maintenon, just southwest of Paris. They are so close and oh so tempting. The French Gothic Chartres Cathedral is another UNESCO World Heritage Site. We are both very interested in visiting it. Before we left home, I booked two nights in Chartres in a renovated, once-grand hotel just across from the train station and centrally located. I also booked a speed train (TGV) from Paris to Bordeaux and then a local train to get to Agen, just north of Condom. We plan to catch a bus from Agen to Condom, where we will resume the Camino. Believe it or not, we can and do plan things—well, sometimes. We don't let *every* station master pick out our itinerary.

Once settled in our room in Chartres, we walk a few blocks over to the Chartres Cathedral, also known as the Cathedrale Notre Dame de Chartres. This beautiful medieval cathedral was first built on the site of a Celtic temple, replaced by a Roman temple, then a Romanesque cathedral. It was finally rebuilt after a fire in the early part of the twelfth century to reflect its current Gothic beauty. Its two magnificent lacy spires come into full view as well as its flying buttresses and its distinctive copper roof turned green. Inside the cathedral, its famous stained glass windows, and particularly, its rose windows, take on a majesty all their own. The blue color in the stained glass, called "*bleu de Chartres*" has never been reproduced since. We pause for a while at the "saint's well" where it is believed early martyrs met their deaths when Vikings destroyed the church in 858. We explore the vast crypt, now famous, that was constructed under Chartres Cathedral afterwards. Emerging from the crypt into the light, we explore the beautiful grounds outside and walk the huge stone labyrinth in the back—Chartres Cathedral's Camino, of sorts.

We stop for lunch in a quaint restaurant across the street, Le Café Serpente—just my kind of place! Whimsical tea pots of all kinds decorate the wide windowsills at the front of the restaurant. *La serveuse* kindly snaps pictures of us at our table—we who are smiling ear to ear, sipping red wine and enjoying our French onion soup and baguettes.

By dusk, we race back to the Cathedral for a light show that is digitally projected across the entire front façade. A crowd has gathered. This is not just any light show. Colorful, fanciful figures dance and twirl and climb the church façade to music. Beautiful images of biblical characters and saints appear next. Later this evening, those nimble figures of light dance once more in my dreams, only now we are all scaling those Cathedral spires together.

At petit déjeuner, we meet a charming French woman, Sylvie. She has become our impromptu guide. She graciously includes us in her walk down narrow cobbled streets to two old churches she herself wants to see, les Églises de Saint Aignan and Saint Pierre. Both are beautiful indeed. We walk back through the oldest section of town past half-timbered medieval houses, one dating back to the twelfth century, and then down the river walk by the Eure. *Merci beaucoup, Madame Sylvie*. Thank you sooo much!

The Château de Maintenon

This morning, we have booked round trip train tickets and are headed to the village of Maintenon, about ten miles away—more specifically, to Françoise d'Aubigné's Château de Maintenon. I am quite fascinated with Madame de Maintenon, the unofficial second wife of Louis XIV, the Sun King. It was a "morganatic" marriage, meaning between royalty or nobility and one of inferior rank, so that no rights of succession to the crown or to property attached to the marriage. Françoise's colorful, tenacious, sometimes controversial, yet inspiring life story is the stuff of novels. And, many have been written about her.

Françoise d'Aubigné was born in Niort, France, on November 27, 1635 at the local prison. Her father, Constant d' Aubigné, the Baron of Surrimeau, found himself jailed at Niort, accused of political treachery. It is here that he met Françoise's mother, the daughter to the prison warden. Upon his release, he moved the family to the West Indies where he accepted a precarious position as governor of Martinique. He died later at Orange, battling the Turks. His death put great hardship on the family. Françoise's mother, struggling with debt, tried unsuccessfully to keep Françoise and her two younger brothers together. But, ultimately, Françoise was sent to her kindly paternal aunt at the Château de Murcay, in Villette. There, she was raised a Protestant. Later, her godmother, Mme. de Neuillant, who cared little for the young girl, made her convert to Catholicism and placed her with the Ursulines, first at Niort, then in Paris.

Faced with the choice between entering the convent or having the stability marriage might bring, Françoise married Paul Scarron. Paul Scarron was a clever and popular figure in the salon circles of the Marais district of Paris. Scarron, a brilliant political satirist and poet, was pitifully deformed, having suffered for years with rheumatism. Historians and novelists alike agree that Françoise, who was much younger than Scarron, was loyal and devoted to him. She, being clever herself, rose in the ranks of society, having learned much from her husband and from the distinguished guests who frequented their home.

Upon Scarron's death, Françoise became the governess to the illegitimate children of Louis XIV. She had been friends, of sorts, with Madame de Montespan, the high-spirited mistress and mother of seven of the King's children. Mme. de Montespan helped her obtain the position of governess. But, it is fair to say, Francoise gained the attention of the King due to her devotion and love for his children, her intelligence, her beauty, and her common sense approach to court politics and intrigue. Upon the death of Queen Maria Theresa of Austria, Françoise married the King in a secret service at Versailles. She remained with him for thirty-two years until he died in 1715. After the King's death, she retired to Saint Cyr to write and to further her support and direction of a school for aristocratic, but impoverished, young ladies, the Maison Royale de Saint-Louis, which she had established with the King's help. She herself died there at the age of eighty-four.

Françoise bought the Château de Maintenon in 1674, intending to live a peaceful country life there, only to find herself, more and more frequently, called back to the King's side at Versailles. At her death, she left the estate to her beloved niece, Charlotte, who had married the Duc de Noailles. The House of Noailles maintained the Château for centuries.

As we step off the train at Maintenon station, we step back in time to seventeenth-century France for a peek into a corner of Françoise's world. I have specially cooked up this visit to Château de Maintenon for our birthday today. We walk for a mile or two toward the village, crossing under the now famous aqueduct built by Louis XIV in his attempt to bring water from the Eure River to his vast gardens and fountains at Versailles. Although the work was ultimately abandoned, the grand old half-completed aqueduct has survived. Today, it stands tall and imposing in the morning mist. It has started to drizzle slightly, and we pick up our pace. As we walk down gray cobblestone streets into the central part of the village, the castle itself looms in full view, complete with its silvery rounded towers, drawbridge, and moat. The little chapel of St. Nicolas, where the King occasionally attended mass with Madame, stands just to the left of the Château. Its gray stone façade glistens in the soft rain. The River Eure flows nearby, next to rows of beautifully pollarded trees. They stand stately, like sentinels from bygone days—it is truly spectacular. I snap pictures quickly for fear I will wake up and it will have all been a dream.

Marcia and I purchase our tickets and cross the drawbridge for a self-guided tour of the Château and its gardens. We walk through the grand gallery and into Madame de Maintenon's library, now renovated. I wonder whether some of her old books and materials on the spiritual principal of "quietude" might still be here as we pass through. The salon du Roi, Louis XIV's bedroom when he sometimes came to visit his wife, is found upstairs in one of the rounded towers. A handsome painting of the King on horseback hangs in the hallway next to his quarters.

The *escalier d'honneur* (grand staircase) leads up to Madame Maintenon's apartments and antechamber, or waiting room. As we are admiring an especially lovely painting of Francoise seated with her niece, we realize, suddenly and simultaneously, just what we are seeing. We have both recognized the beautiful picture just behind Françoise in the painting. It is The Annunciation, by Philippe de Champaigne. I happen to have that very same painting of the Blessed Mary and the dove hanging above my bed back home. It is a charming reproduction painted by one of my friends. "You could have been Madame de Maintenon," Marcia exclaims. And the truth is, I feel a deep kindred spirit with Françoise, beyond words. More than anything else, Marcia and I appreciate the gentle synchronicity of the moment. As we wind our way back down the staircase, both of us are lost in our own thoughts. Oh, the sweet silence of awe.

As we prepare to leave the Château, we come upon a massive painting of Françoise located in a small outer room on the first floor, all to itself. It is hauntingly beautiful. Françoise is lying in her bed at St. Cyr, the sisters peering out from a curtain nearby as a certain visitor drops down on one knee before her. He is Tsar Peter I of Russia, who has come to meet her and to pay his respects. Our tour at an end, we reluctantly pass back across the moat and emerge into the twenty-first century once again.

By now, we are hungry and head across the street to a restaurant for pizza before we walk back to the station. It is late afternoon and time to return to our hotel at Chartres.

Ce matin, we are headed back to Paris Gare Montparnasse, changing to the TGV to Bordeaux, to Agen, and then back by bus to Condom, where we had left the Camino the year before. It is such a simple pleasure to ride the trains and buses, especially when we know that travel *à pied* will soon commence in earnest. By now it is old home week with the woman in Condom who owns the British market—we stock up on supplies. She says she remembers us from the year before. Maybe so, though I am not so sure if this is good or bad—we, the rather scroungy pèlerines. "Oh no, here they come again!" Or maybe it's the twin thing. We forget about being identical twins until we notice someone staring at us—*les jumelles identiques*. Having inquired about gîtes for the night, we amble across the commerce district and down past the river to a large privately-owned gîte d'étape on the Camino leaving Condom. We have gotten to this ancient stone refuge too late to reserve the pilgrim meal already being prepared by our host, but we settle in with our pasta marina we have cooked up, happy as two little clams. At least we have beds. *À demain!* Yes, until tomorrow!

A crisp, cool morning greets us. Today, we have set our sights on the village of Montréal-du-Gers, eleven miles away. It feels so good to be back on the Camino. It is raw and almost surreal. After about six miles, down grassy lanes and through woods and fields, we reach the ancient Église de Routges. This is a beautiful little stone church with its exceedingly interesting side entrance. That entrance was reserved for a certain group of shunned people in the region in the Middle Ages, the Cagots. We have to stoop low to get through the small narrow door. It is unimaginable, the misery and indignity these people must have suffered, perhaps not unlike the black slaves of our sordid past. There is some speculation that these people were lepers, or beggars, or all manner of ill. Fear, whether real or imagined, fuels injustice, then and now. The interior of the church is quite lovely with its rendition of the Blessed Mary and Jesus. Low wooden benches, candles, and flowers are set out all around. We linger here for a long while.

By the time we walk into Montréal-du-Gers, we are both tired and looking for a place for the night. We stop in at one gîte that is supposed to be a popular place, but would that have been several years ago? The kitchen is swarming with flies, and the bedrooms offer little relief from them either. Marcia is amazed and upset that I would even consider staying here. Well, I was trying to give it a chance. We hurry on, trying not to look back. Closer in the village, we come upon another gîte. Its friendly "meeter and greeter" is out looking for us too. Yes, a small scruffy dog is barking excitedly and running in and out of an open door to a private gîte d'étape clamoring for our business, I guess. And thus, we meet Vicki the dog who is part of the welcoming committee. We book for the night and are led up steep stairs to a large rectangular room. Single beds, bright coral-colored blankets neatly folded on each one, line both long walls—a "sight for sore eyes," as mother would say. Now, we meet the second half of the welcoming committee, on duty upstairs and strolling through our dormitory room, Cerise (Cherry) the cat. Marcia immediately sprawls out on one of the little beds like she has come home while I snap her picture, along with shots of you-know-who—Vicki and Cherise.

Our host will serve petit déjeuner tomorrow morning, but we are on our own for dinner. We end up walking across the village square to a cozy restaurant for an early meal and then return for bed. We are decidedly back into our rhythm and routine—Camino style. As I pull my blanket up around my shoulders, I settle in to plot our course for tomorrow. Marcia is doing the same, until we both soon fall into deep sleep. *Bonne nuit!*

The fresh green of spring is everywhere. This day, the Camino takes us down a narrow dirt trail through lush woods and overhanging trees. It is as though we are walking through a dark tunnel. A luminous circle of light glimmers in the distance—it is beautiful. As we come out the other end, we find ourselves in a wide yellow expanse of canola flowers, as far as the eye can see—more beauty still. It feels almost like *a near-death experience* might, except that we are still in the physical and not the ethereal realms. If this is so, I am reluctant to return from whence I came. But the bubble bursts, as it always must in the physical world sooner or later, as we walk on. Well, actually *sooner*, as you will soon see.

Apparently, it has rained a lot in this area, for as we approach a low-lying section near a stream, the going gets muddy. By now, we have met up with Susan, an English woman who is traveling the Camino *seule*, by herself. She speaks a little French, and we are about to get a French lesson we won't soon forget. 'What's the name for mud?" I ask curiously. With that, she belts it out: "Boo hoo—it's *boue*." And we pick up the snappy refrain from there, all three of us slipping and slogging merrily through the mud singing our new tune, *tous les trios*. I will never need to

Resting spot at the church at Lanne-Soubiran

ask again the word for mud, much less how to pronounce it. We tromp through *boue* (and probably poo and doo) for what seems like two miles. Susan, who walks slightly faster than we do, finally goes on. We sit down and attempt to clean off our boots, heavy with—now you know the word too—*boue*.

Not soon enough, we get to the large town of Eauze. We have walked almost ten miles, plenty for us today. Serendipitously, we have stopped in at the old split-timbered Café de France, a landmark for the village. Susan also happens to be there. She has already claimed a room located nearby. We agree to meet back at the café for an early dinner. The bartender walks us down a cobbled side street with some keys to a room upstairs, where we have now also booked. Before even considering heading out again to explore the town, we have to wash the caked *boue* off of our hiking pants and boots and take showers.

Later, we meet up with Susan as planned, and all of us order *steak-frites et une salade verte*—a popular dish in France, we are told. *Oui, c'est tres delicieux!* The café is bustling with business, locals and pilgrims alike. After dinner, we walk over to the Gothic Cathedral of Saint Luperc, a national monument. I am not prepared for its beauty. I wonder just what would move the Benedictine community to construct such a place as this for their local saint? Saint Luperculus was a martyred bishop from the third century. I can find little else about him on the internet. Still musing, I wonder what might be recorded about him in the Book of Life or in the Akashic Records since nothing is lost to God. It is only lost to me, for now. I am reminded of what King David wrote in the Psalms: "Thou tellest my wanderings: put thou my tears into thy bottle: are they not in thy book?" Psalms 56:8

It would be quite dark inside, but for the Cathedral's magnificent rose window and its brilliantly colored, long, narrow stained glass windows. Shafts of light are pouring into the nave, reflecting the light of the setting sun. They beam what look like dancing spheres of ethereal pink and orange and blue all the way down the center aisle. They are heavenly orbs—*magnifique!* We recognize St. Roch and his dog in one of the stained glass windows. St. Roch is dressed in purple, cockle shells on his cape. He is holding his staff and gourd in one hand. The other hand is reaching out to a woman who is most likely suffering from the plague. She is lying on the ground before him, her children and husband surrounding her, hoping and praying, it seems, for a miracle. It is mesmerizing, as though we were there looking on too. An equally beautiful, colorful image of St. Jacques is portrayed on another stained glass panel nearby.

Dark metal chandeliers hang low from the tall ceiling. Just to dazzle us more, lovely old paintings of Jesus and the Blessed Mary shine forth in the dim light. In one painting, Mary is assumed into heaven, dark clouds and an orange-red glow surrounding her. She is crowned in a golden halo of twelve stars. I am reminded of Revelations 12:1, where it is written: "And there appeared a great wonder in heaven: a woman clothed with the sun, and the moon under her feet, and upon her head a crown of twelve stars." I just want to sit down and cry—it is all so stunning.

We have breakfast early, at the Café de France, and head out planning to reach Nogaro by late afternoon. I feel suspended in time as we plod along. So, let us consider cycles of time and rest. Back home, I had been running like a little rat on a wheel. One night, after an especially busy week at work, I ate dinner early and climbed into bed to watch the news, only to fall straight away into a deep sleep. The television blaring and the lights still on, I woke up startled and leaped up. It was daylight. I glanced at my smart phone and realized that it was twenty minutes before eight o'clock, and I was about to miss an important meeting. I threw on my clothes, gulped down a cup of cold coffee, and drove over to the office. All the way over, I was thinking in despair, *How could I have slept twelve hours like that?* When I got there, there were no cars in the parking lot. Let's see now—what is wrong with this picture? It reminded me of a segment from the "Twilight Zone," except that I had oddly found myself in the middle of it. Totally disoriented, I checked my watch again. You guessed it, eight o'clock in the evening. I had slept two hours, not twelve hours. I drove back home, greatly relieved that I actually had a full night ahead of me to collect myself, rest, and revitalize. To be jolted out of the cycle of time sometimes can be a good thing. It is as though I was transported through a warp in time's fabric and into the *now* in slow, conscious motion, until time virtually stood still.

As we are making our way towards Nogaro this morning, I find myself suspended in time once more, as I manage to put one foot in front of the other, trudging down the path. I am noticing scrubby bushes and tall trees, a powder blue sky, birds chirping, and the gentle breeze on my face. I am also quick to notice those little snails, and I am careful not to step on them, as I pass them by. The pungent, earthy smell of dirt and woods is intensified. I see my world and my place in it in this beautiful *now*. And the Camino smiles back, as it is observing me. I too am smiling *dans ce moment*. I have no thoughts, only walking and freedom and peace.

Marcia suddenly jars me back into the flow of time as we approach a detour for the Église-Hôpital Sainte-Chrisite. "Should we go this way?" she is asking with consternation and urgency. It takes a lot for us to manage a detour. This one does not disappoint. As we draw near the church, it is as though we are hearing the music of the spheres, so lovely is the sound. The soulful sound of what I think may be a lute is calling us to drop our heavy packs, come in, and rest—if only for a little while. We oblige. Once inside, we see that two musicians are practicing for a public performance that is to be held there later that evening. *Ça tombe bien*. Our timing is perfect. Other pilgrims have gathered too, and we experience our own mini concert under the dancing light of a huge crystal chandelier. After a while, we leave and make our way along regaining the Camino. Don't forget to take those detours in life. It is those shortcuts you have to be wary of, unless they are by divine appointment.

Nogaro is a large, spread-out town. We get to the village square and find all the rooms are taken. We walk back and up another street, in the heat, to a large public gîte which we hope will be available. It too is full. We are bemoaning the fact that we have wasted time and energy and several miles now looking for beds for the night. We are both tired and a little confounded, not to mention a little cranky. Well, I should speak for myself. At one point, a man who is a bit inebriated, but clearly in distress, comes running out of his shop and stops us on the street. He tearfully explains that his young adult daughter was killed in an automobile accident a few years before. He asks that we pray for her as we walk the Camino. We assure him that we will, but that we will mostly be praying for *him*—for a father who must let go and move on, if only for his daughter who would want him to be happy, or at least at peace. It is a poignant moment. He thanks us profusely and then directs us another mile up the street and off the Camino to where we might find a room. It is a nice hotel located on the motorway just outside Nogaro. We are able to book there—clean beds and sheets and towels. I hardly know how to act. And who should we meet up with at dinner in the hotel restaurant but our new British friend Susan whom we met in the mud—aka *Madame Boue*. There is much good cheer and debriefing around the table until we all finally head up for bed. Nothing was wasted anywhere this day.

Six miles into our route this morning, we have stopped for a rest at a church at Lanne-Soubiran. Its wide porch offers us some much-needed shade as I suspect it has for many other pilgrims before us. The fragrance of roses fills the air. This is a beautiful old church. Its octagonal ceiling has been painted dark blue with tiny twinkling stars all around. A dove, symbolizing the Holy Spirit, is encircled in swirling white clouds at the center of the ceiling just over the altar. The stained glass windows glow softly with the noonday sun. A feeling of peace has permeated the nave and has graciously wrapped its arms around us too. It is hard to leave it. But back outside once more, I have plopped down on the bench by the door to rest my weary feet. Marcia is busy taking photos of the rosebush by the porch, its branches drooping with ruby red roses. This is our self-designated picnic spot, and we dine on fresh tomatoes and sardines and crackers. And, did I forget the chocolate bar and the lemon wafers? A kindly gentleman walks over from next door and joins us. He and his wife, who are both Brits, have remodeled a gîte d'étape that they hope to open soon. He is the unofficial friend and keeper of the church. He doesn't have to say it—I just know. I make a mental note that I must preserve this charming old church for myself in a painting, and so I snap pictures all the way up the long walkway as we leave it.

We want to spend the night in Barcelonne-du-Gers. We will have walked almost seventeen miles today. I am promising my feet and my back that we will go no farther today. Once finally there, we happen upon a lovely gîte just behind a private home. It is the Gîte du Cosset. The property is surrounded by an ornate white-iron fence. We ring the bell and are let inside. The first level of the gîte has a pleasant kitchen and a long table with chairs where our breakfast will be set out the next morning. I also notice a small simple painting of Jesus and the woman at the well. It is so lovely that I am transfixed by it. *La Madame*, who is cheerful and kind, escorts us upstairs to one of the small rooms. It has two little twin beds (forgive the pun). She has given us bright green plastic baskets in which to organize our things; it is quite sweet really. Later, we walk over to a restaurant that caters to both pilgrims and locals alike. I order the pilgrim meal and choose *le poisson, des frites, et une salade verte*. Marcia chooses the same: fish, fries, and a green salad. I never order fries back home, but I have thrown caution to the wind tonight. Back at the gîte, I am drifting off into a starry night's sleep right in the middle of something Marcia is trying to tell me. God only knows what it was.

Out early again this morning, we leave the village of Barcelonne-du-Gers and very soon reach its companion town of Aire-sur-l'Adour. As we approach, the long bridge over the Rive de l'Adour is lined with traffic. Cars are bumper-to-bumper going slowly. We walk past them on the sidewalk over the bridge. Colorful flags from all nations are mounted all along the bridge, waving in the breeze, saluting those who are coming in and out of town. I am happily carrying on, oblivious to the downward swoop of a very large stork who was trying to clear the cars. Marcia yells. It barely missed my head. Ignorance is bliss, sometimes. Marcia is just glad that stork didn't swoop down on *her*. We find a large supermarket and stock up on cat food, almonds, dark chocolate, yogurt, bananas, apples, and water—the essentials.

We then stop for awhile at the twelfth-century Cathedral of Saint-Jean Baptiste. This is another particularly beautiful old church, its walls painted in scenes from the Bible in peach and green and aqua. The high rounded ceiling and the nave fairly glow in the subdued golden light. An emblem of the Lamb of God blazes on the top of the ceiling. This is a perfect place for us to rest and pray. I think that all of my life's journey is a prayer, really. Walking the Camino is a prayer. How could it be otherwise? A kindly priest is at the back stamping pilgrim passports—ours included.

Moving along yet again, we find ourselves walking up a seemingly never-ending steep sidewalk through the upper reaches of the town. We are walking steadily up and up and up. I am in my element. Marcia lags behind, until she speeds by me on the rocky passage downhill, through the woods. I am not interested in another mishap with my ankle. I am taking it slowly and carefully, although this is certainly not a guarantee of anything.

We finally reach Miramont-Sensacq. We are able to stay at the municipal gîte for ten euros and a donation for the dinner and petit déjeuner in the morning. Pilgrims from Holland and Iceland have stopped here too. They are all English speakers, including our soon-to-be new Dutch friend, Leafre. I am most excited to make claim to my bunk bed and to crawl quietly into it after dinner—squatter's rights.

It is a cool and humid and hazy morning. Rain is heading our way—you can smell it. We are now approaching the Departement of the Pyrénées-Atlantiques. The scenery is changing. We are hiking through lush green fields and farmland and across rolling hills. We are also afforded our first view of the Pyrenees, their snow-capped peaks looming in the distance in the mist. We are getting a preview of what we will soon enough be crossing. About three miles farther, we reach the eleventh-century Église de Sensacq. It is another splendid old church with its steeple and its terracotta tiled roof. This one has a lovely old cemetery in the enclosed yard just behind the church. It offers up a good place for a rest.

We stop again at the church of Saint Barthelemy in Pimbo. Pimbo is in the Departement de Landes, in the Aquitaine region of southwestern France. In the church, we find a magnificent red and gold stained glass window of Mary. Her flowing robe is sky blue. She stands on top of the world among the clouds. She is trampling the snake, a familiar image by now in some of these ancient Camino churches. As we leave the church, it is beginning to rain. And, coming into the large town of Arzacq-Arraziguet, the sky opens up a deluge. Fortunately, we find shelter for the night at a large gîte d'étape in the central part of the village. Other pilgrims there are buzzing with talk of a welcoming social for the pilgrims commencing soon, across the way at the parish church of Saint Pierre. We quickly drop our bags in our room and rush over in the rain, and dare I leave out that I fall flat on the slippery pavement as I am hastily entering the church. No broken bones. It is a not-so-subtle reminder to slow down. The parish women greet us with biscuits and tea. Clearly, it is their gracious mission in service to those on the Camino.

I can't help but notice the most delightful shining countenance of a silver-haired pèlerine. Folks surrounding her are most likely basking in her bright light. We meet this fascinating woman again at dinner around a long crowded table of fellow pilgrims. Jacqueline, who is in her eighties, is walking the Camino. She is also just freshly back from running a half-marathon. She explains as best she can in half French and half English that her doctor has advised her to cut down on her usual running activities—full marathons (twenty-six miles). "I just love to run!" she says cheerfully. It is enough to put the rest of us to shame. Running is such a positive addiction and an opportunity for active meditation. I suspect that walking the Camino is one as well. What is illumination anyway? Is it a spiritual awakening or a quickening? I suspect one cannot grasp for it or want it too much, for like other things in life that are held too closely, it will only elude. Oh that I would shine brightly too someday—she is so lovely.

We leave Arzacq-Arraziguet bright and early this morning along a narrow street in the village, the Chemin de Saint-Jacques. Not too far along the Camino, we have the good fortune to meet one Monsieur Arbre de Pèlerin—a huge old tree who is as wide as he is tall. He looks like he has been standing around motionless eating croissants au chocolat nonstop for the last thirty years, at least—his girth is so wide. His grand knotty crevices are filled with candles and scallop shells and prayer notes and even a little statue of Mary. Oh, and, of course, hot pink plastic flowers are tucked under one of his many leafy arms. Pilgrims have lovingly loaded him up. As if this were not enough, a line of shells runs up one side of his ancient trunk. A sign posted on him reads "*arbre du pèlerin.*" I wonder if he is a cousin of Treebeard from the land of hobbits, what the elves call an *ent*. If trees could smile, this stately old gentleman most surely must be smiling right about now. His grin stretches all across his gnarly old face. And, I think that I notice a slight wink as we pass him by. "*Enchanté, Monsieur Arbre. Enchanté!*" We are grinning too now, ear-to-ear, as we stumble on down the Camino hardly able to contain ourselves.

We rest for a while at the church at Louvigny and sit in the shade of its cool dark porch with our Dutch friend, Leafre, before pressing on. This church has a modern, quite pretty stained glass window of a nun holding a bouquet of roses. Yellow and pink and red roses encircle her against a backdrop of sky blue. More than five miles later, we reach the Romanesque Church of Saint Pierre at the village of Larreule. This beautiful church sits high on a grassy hill—it was an important site for pilgrims in the Middle Ages. A huge sparkling chandelier hangs from the high ceiling in the interior, casting specks of light onto rows and rows of old wooden benches in the nave. An image of Jesus is suspended behind the altar with red and gold framed paintings of some of the saints. We are quite fortunate to be able to visit these ancient churches which have generously opened their doors to parishioners and pilgrims alike.

We are ready to stop for the day soon and wish to find shelter at the village of Uzan. The problem is—the only *gîte* there is full. There is little else to offer us for the night if we continue along on the Camino. This is where our friend Leafre fits into the picture. Marcia is now calling her "Gold Leaf." Rightly so! Leafre, who has already reserved a bed for herself at this *gîte* now full, is busy asking the Madame in French where we too might possibly stay for the night, since it is ominously closing in on nightfall. "*Attendez!* "Madame exclaims excitedly. We are to wait as she calls up her sister who lives nearby. Within thirty minutes, her dearest sister rides up on her bicycle and escorts us down the street a few blocks to her own home. She has made space for us, as well as for an elderly man, another pilgrim who also needs help quickly. Cecile has a large, beautiful brick home where she lives with her teenage son—her husband is deceased. We are given an upstairs bedroom. And later, after showers, we come down to the kitchen where she has prepared a most wonderful meal—pasta marinara, green salads, crusty *baguettes*, and *mousse au chocolat*. She joins us for dinner, and we converse as best we can, laugh, and take pictures around her kitchen table. The experience brings tears to my eyes even as I write this. It is just one more example of the kindness and the gentle hospitality shown us as pilgrims along the Way. By divine appointment, I feel quite sure.

"*Au revoir et merci beaucoup!*" I turn and call out one last time as we leave Cecile this cool morning. We have almost fourteen miles we plan to go today. We hope to reach the Église d'Argagnon and a private gîte before the sun sets. By late afternoon, however, we have walked through the last town and still haven't found the gîte, until we find a small sign for it at the end of the village. We veer off the paved road and are now walking down a dirt road and through the woods, seemingly endlessly. I am starting to second-guess the sign we saw which is never good, and I wonder if we have taken a wrong turn. We finally reach a clearing and a large farmhouse and surrounding buildings. Dogs are barking excitedly. A man comes out to meet us waving and smiling (always a good sign) signaling that we have made it to the right place. He gives us single beds in a small building behind the main house. The beds are all taken now for the night. The group we met before from Iceland is here too. By early evening, we are served dinner as our host sits and smiles, strumming his banjo. He is particularly interested in Marcia and me because he loves the folk tunes and the bluegrass music of the South in the States. We have found another spot of gracious accommodation on our path. Or did it find us?

We plan to get to the large bastide town of Navarrenx today. It is a town fortified by ramparts (wide stone walls) by a river. We have walked another fourteen miles. We just want to get there *sans* too many blisters. Unfortunately, we can find no beds and end up walking two more kilometers off the Camino to find room at the Gîte Charbel on the other side of town. This must be what impatience gets you (or should I say *me*). We are lucky to be here. This gîte, dedicated to Saint Charbel, is quite nice. I am not familiar with this saint, so I read about him: Saint Charbel, called "the wonderworker of the East," was a nineteenth-century Lebanese monk, priest, and finally, a hermit. A few months after his death, his tomb was surrounded in bright light, and when he was exhumed, his body was found to be uncorrupted. Our host at the gîte, as well as thousands of others who make intercessory prayers to Saint Charbel, claim miraculous cures and help in their lives. What I like best about this holy man is that for the last twenty-six years of his life, he withdrew from the world into a life of deep prayer and contemplation. I realize most individuals are called to be active participants in the world, which is as it should be. But there are those, both men and women, who are called to be spiritual anchors—he being one, Saint Teresa of Avila, another. Were they enlightened first, or did they turn within and therein find the light through their mystical practices? I have gotten off the Camino again, but maybe not too far.

I am reminded of what happened to me a few years ago, after a month or so of meditating on the Greek Orthodox Jesus Prayer "Lord Jesus Christ, have mercy on me." I was busy as usual, and when I stepped out of my car one morning to get to an appointment, I looked down, and at my feet lying in the dirt face up was the most beautiful little enamel pendant of Jesus that I have ever seen. It is as though Jesus handed it over to me for my efforts. Of course, one of my friends simply remarked that it was an example of the law of attraction—what you think about and focus on is what you get. Thoughts are things. Perhaps there is some truth in this, but, I suspect, probably not the whole truth. The Jesus Prayer, also called the Prayer of the Heart, is considered to be the unceasing prayer that the Apostle Paul wrote of in the New Testament, a method of opening the heart. I see the blazing crimson hearts of Mary and of Jesus everywhere in the art and paintings in the old churches on the Camino. They are not lost to me. And, along the Camino, I pray the Prayer of Jesus sometimes, or should I say the Prayer prays me, for I am lost in its mysteries soon enough. Then, I am reminded of my wish when we started the Camino: *Oh that Jesus would walk with me*, and I look down and see that my pendant is indeed resting gently at my heart as we press on.

Leaving Navarrenx this morning, we have to retrace our steps back through the town to get back onto the Camino. This is the area of the Bearn in the southern rolling hills. Homes are characteristically constructed of pebbles and stone and cob. We are also moving into Basque country and into the foothills of the Pyrenees. By the time we reach the small village of Lichos, we have walked about ten miles. We eventually find a room in a family home just after the town which has beds for pilgrims. Had the dogs been better cared for there, I would have been more content, but two of the dogs were tied up by doghouses on four-foot ropes with no shade. The third is a house dog who has never been groomed. Its hair lies in clumps on its back. Yes, we may be called spoiled Americans, and I do realize that many dogs in our country have the same troubling fate. I just don't like to see it—neglect of man or beast.

Three miles farther along this morning, we stop at the Romanesque church of Saint-Étienne in Aroue. This is another old church, its ceiling painted heather green with stars all around. As we turn to leave it, we look up to the choir loft to find a lovely image of Mary in white robes and a blue sash. The morning sun is shining through a small circular stained glass window. It softly

The Église Notre Dame and the Porte d'Espagne in
Saint-Jean-Pied-de-Port

illumines her. Our backpacks and poles are propped up at the door—we take them up again and walk on.

Past Aroue, our walking guide gives us the option of taking a slightly shorter route to Uhart-Mixe known as the snail route. Sign me up! Sure enough, leaving town we come upon a sign with a snail and take that route—Marcia *et moi*, the two snails. Perhaps this is the time to say it. Marcia and I walk slower than almost anyone else. No matter how we try to pick up our speed, our fellow pèlerins pass us by. Marcia keeps telling me (like a broken record) to take shorter, quicker steps. I try this approach, but with no real progress. But we, who are determined snails, manage to pass those who have stopped longer for their lunches and breaks. I notice (rather self-righteously) that we all get to the gîtes by early evening just the same. I am getting a little punchy by now. "Don't you dare call me a *slug!*" I laugh. Marcia, however, having already tuned me out, is heading further up the trail in front of me. Yes, at a *snail's pace*—just like me.

Today it is hot, and the sun is unrelenting with little shade anywhere. We are walking along dirt roads by vast fields and farmland. It feels to me like we are a bit lost, since we are finding few waymarks in this area of the Camino. We finally just sit down by the side of the road for our picnic lunch of energy bars and peanuts—and *this* is the shortcut. We eventually reach *la petite village d'Uhart-Mixe* and find beds at, where else but, Le Gîte de l'Escargot. It is a true refuge in the Bearn—the Gîte of the Snail. This is a large, attractive white-washed gîte d'étape and bar with brown shutters; it is typical of some of the beautiful houses in the Basque region. Tables and chairs are set outside under inviting brightly colored umbrellas. They have thought of everything to make their guests more comfortable. A young woman has a horse tied up, grazing, nearby, and she is feeding and stroking him. We won't be worrying about *him*. After we unpack and repack and shower, Marcia and I walk just across the road to their lovely old church. Its colorful stained glass windows form a half circle above the altar. The ceiling is a pretty shade of dark blue-green.

At dinner, our gracious hosts have arranged their pilgrim guests family style around a long table in the dining room. The walls are painted a warm peachy color. It is all charming. We are served vegetable soup followed by a platter *de la viande* (some sort of meat), pasta, *les salades*, *le vin rouge*, crusty baguettes, *fromage*, and *une mousse au choolat* for dessert. By nightfall, I am almost asleep before I can reach my little bed. Marcia and I are situated upstairs and share a room with several male pèlerins—pilgrim style, you might say. We exchange greetings, none of us concerned about a sleeping arrangement which would raise eyebrows in the States. Just glad to have a bed are we. Our room is painted in more happy hues of orange.

By morning's light, the walls fairly glow with the rising sun beaming through our window. We are getting anxious to get to Saint-Jean-Pied-de-Port and are counting the kilometers again this morning. We are also entering the most northern part of French Basque Country, with its own distinctive language, cultural heritage, and cuisine. But first, we have breakfast. Petit dejeuner has been set out beautifully in the dining room: fresh-squeezed orange juice, yogurt, toasted baguettes, and croissants. Their hospitality knows no bounds.

As we leave Uhart-Mixe, we are climbing uphill and down again on paved roads by farms and grassy fields. The hazy mountains in the distance beckon us toward them. We are walking in rolling countryside now. Horses are grazing just off the path. Chickens running around close by them are too far away to cause Marcia any alarm. We pass two ancient stone crosses. Pilgrims have placed pebbles and stones at their base. It is, most likely, a way to mark their passage. We are approaching Ostabat-Asme, a small village that is nestled in the lush green valley before us. As we round the corner down the cobblestone street into the town, a man is sitting at a picnic table reading a paper in front of a small shop. A little cat is peeking up over the edge of the table, sitting right next to him—I guess, hoping for a handout. The man doesn't seem to notice, but, of course, we do. The shop keeper doesn't sell cat food. Luckily, we still have some. And you know the tale from here. Kitty is quite ravenous and manages to eat a whole tin of fishy feline food as we sit resting and watching her. I guess the mice pickings are pretty slim today.

We are planning to get to the village of Larceveau and to stay at the Hotel Espellet, which our guidebook recommends as a good place to find lodging. We have about three more miles to go. As we carry on, we find ourselves walking on a narrow grassy pathway into dense woods and low, overhanging trees. Then, suddenly, it seems that we are into another time tunnel. A bright sphere of light at the end of this leafy tunnel is leading us down the Camino to who-knows-where-or-when. I love these dark passages into the light—this one is rather surreal. We finally emerge from the undergrowth and find ourselves standing in front of a tall white cross. More pebbles, courtesy of the pilgrims, have been stacked on the top of its base. It is a grand old cross overlooking the hills and the snowy mountain tops looming now just beyond. This is a good place for a rest. I suspect many others have sat down in the dirt here too. We are both stretched out, only too happy to rest and to gaze up at the clouds as they drift by. *Are they traveling the Camino too?*

Unfortunately, the patisserie in Larceveau is closed. I was so much hoping for an éclair or croissant au chocolat or something else equally sinful. The Hotel Espellet is just down the roadway and across the street. We are near Saint-Jean—the traffic is picking up. We cross over and book a room with dinner and petit déjeuner—pilgrim fare. The hotel caters to pilgrims and to motor travelers alike. After we unpack, we walk for awhile behind the hotel down a quaint residential area of the town. Who would have thought we had any more energy for walking again this day—certainly not our feet. But it is warm and balmy and early in the afternoon, and walking seems just the ticket.

The hotel serves a traditional and tasty Basque dish of grilled fish and mild red peppers as part of their pilgrim menu this evening. It is eight o'clock, and I am again counting the miles for our journey tomorrow. We will be hiking for about ten miles along a path just off the road, passing through several hamlets and the village of Saint-Jean-le-Vieux, and then into Saint-Jean-Pied-de Port (Donibane Garazi in the Basque language). This is the end of our trip for this segment of the Camino.

But not so fast! This morning, we awake to a light cold drizzle. The rain only intensifies as we wind steadily up the trail. Oh, to be a bird and fly away. But, oh no, the joy of going pilgrim-style is that we get to slip and slide and slog along a high narrow footpath, the woods on one side and the cars whizzing by on the other. It is still raining slightly as we get to Saint-Jean-Pied-de Port, but we are too excited to notice. We have crossed over a bridge and are walking up the Chemin Saint-Jacques in the mist, about to enter the old walled village. This beautiful little Basque village is nestled in the foothills of the snow-peaked Pyrenees. The lush bluish-green mountains in the distance form a spectacular backdrop to the town. It is as though we are walking in the clouds, they are so low. We pose for pictures of ourselves just before the Porte Saint-Jacques. Marcia is standing here shivering and clutching her rain cape around her in the wind. I am faring no better. But our big smiles seem to say it all.

Saint-Jean-Pied-de-Port (St-Jean at the Foot of the Pass) is surrounded by ramparts. We pass through the Port Saint-Jacques with its thick walls and into the town, then continue down the Rue de la Citadelle until we soon reach the municipal gîte and pilgrim information center on the right. Fellow pilgrims are already lined up outside the entrance. We join the lines. It is mid-afternoon, and we are all angling for beds for the night. We get a sense the gîte here is filling up fast, but Marcia doesn't want to stay here anyway, thinking we might find better options closer into the central part of town. *Bonne chance!* (Good luck!) Saint-Jean-Pied-de-Port is a bustling and important convergence for the three routes on the Camino coming from France. It is also the starting point for many who walk the main route, the Camino Frances, through Spain only. *Busy* is the operative word here.

After waiting in line, our harried questions patiently answered and our passports stamped, we carry on down the steep cobblestone street. And a delightful street it is! Charming shops and cafes and gîtes are everywhere. But, oh dear, the gîtes are either closed until late afternoon, or full, or both, per the signs posted on their doors. Pots of red and pink posies and trumpet vines overhanging the street wave us on.

At the bottom of Rue de la Citadelle, we stop for a while at the Gothic Church of Notre-Dame-du-bout-du-pont (Our Lady at the end of the bridge). This beautiful fourteenth-century church sits at the Porte d'Espagne, by the bridge over the Nive River. Inside, rows and rows of long, white, tapered candles and red votives, all aglow, are set out near the altar—their light piercing the cool darkness. The sweet smell of incense, candles, and lilies fills the air. All manner of prayer notes are tucked into recesses under a statue of Mary and the Baby Jesus at the front. The long windows of stained glass are working their magic too, casting a beautiful subtle shimmer over it all. Despite a sense of urgency that we are feeling to find lodging, we sit for a spell. After all, we are at a pivotal place on the Camino at this holy refuge, where many others have rested too and sought shelter and solace and aid through the ages. If these old pink stone walls, oozing with history and tales of the Camino, could only tell us what they know.

For over an hour, we continue to look for a place to stay. We have doubled back now, and as we trudge back up the Rue de Citadelle, the one and only "Madame Camino" herself is standing outside her door inviting us to come in. As we soon discover, Madame Camino, a veritable fixture on the Camino, offers rooms to pèlerins at her *chambres d'hôte*. A small sign, posted high above the door decorated with a scallop shell, reads *"Chez l'Habitant."* How did we miss it? Thankfully, she has a vacancy, and she kindly shows us up four flights of stairs to our room. She has given us a room with a double bed. Our private bathroom is outside, however, just out the back door and off the balcony—no problem for us. We are afforded a lovely bird's eye view over the terracotta rooftops and gardens of the village. And, we are higher than the rampart in the distance. People are walking it even now as we look down on them.

We unpack and then head out again to explore the village and to find a restaurant for an early dinner. It has stopped raining. The streets are not so crowded now, and many of the shops are just re-opening. We climb steep stone stairs and walk the rampart ourselves in the dusk of early evening—we have another splendid view of the village. We also tour the old citadel nearby. At dinner, we both order a delicious calamari salad that is one of the best I have had anywhere. But as the sun sets a damp cold settles in, signaling it is time to head back quickly.

Did I mention we have no heat in our room? By now, Marcia and I have put on every single stitch of clothing we can dig out of our backpacks, and still, we shiver in our bed, made worse by the occasional bathroom run outside in the chilly air. And did I say that I am grateful to be here? Actually, I am, but I pass on a shower in the morning. It is just too darn cold. As we head out for breakfast, we manage to get into somewhat of a squabble with Madame Camino, who is simply trying to tell us in French that she has to go out early this morning for a hair appointment and that she has to lock the door. Marcia thinks she is trying to charge us more for the room and starts to get upset. I am not far behind her. We find someone to translate, and with some amount of doleful apologies on our part and smiles all around, we leave. All in a day for dear patient Madame Camino, I guess, dealing with us pilgrims—year, after year, after year.

But there is no looking back, as more adventure awaits us. We are hoping to book a train to the Basque port city of Bayonne, which is just over thirty miles northwest and near the Atlantic coast. The train station in Saint-Jean-Pied-de-Port is several blocks away on the other side of town, but within walking distance. And just who are we kidding anyway—we who walk everywhere? We walk over. We are lucky to have snagged two train tickets this morning, for this railway station is a big hub for pilgrims coming and going on the Camino. Today, we are glad to go. It is time. Saint-Jean-Pied-de-Port—*quelle belle ville!* We will return to you *encore une fois*, once again next year.

We arrive in Bayonne quickly and are assessing the cityscape from the Gare de Bayonne, hoping to locate a good hotel nearby. Looking just to the left as we cross the street, we find the Hotel Côte Basque and settle in there. The hotel staff is friendly and helpful. They point us just up the street to the Pont Saint-Esprit, where we can walk across the Adour River to go into central Bayonne, called the Grand Bayonne district.

Bayonne, which sits at the mix of the Adour and Nive Rivers, has a rich and varied history. It was once ruled by the Romans and then later by the British, after Henry II of England married Eleanor of Aquitaine in 1152. In the early sixteenth century, the town experienced a terrible bout with the plague which decimated the population. Interestingly, I am also learning more about Bayonne's connection to the Camino. It seems the Way of Bayonne is a route on the Camino coming from the coastal villages to join the Camino Frances at Pamplona, just across the Pyrenees in Spain. British pilgrims also take this route to join up on the Camino coming from England.

It is a sunny and breezy late morning as we cross the Saint-Esprit Bridge and then walk over to the city central. We are excited to see the city, lovely Bayonne, with its colorful shops and cafes and its Gothic Cathedral. We sit for a while in the church and then nose in and out of the stores up and down the cobbled streets before we head back across the bridge to the hotel.

It is an adjustment not to be following waymarks now that we are off the Camino. I catch myself looking down for them just the same. In larger towns on the Camino, one might find brass shells embedded in the sidewalks marking a clear path through the hustle and bustle of the city. And, speaking of *waymarks*, just what does mark our passage or guide us through our lives? I wish I had had yellow shells or red and white balises to guide me and to help me make the choices I made, especially in my younger years. I would have appreciated those Xs drawn on trees to warn me I was heading in the wrong direction. Of course, most likely, those signals came in other ways. I have just chosen to ignore them. I decidedly feel I have made poor choices sometimes—we all have. But, I see now that errant choices were corrected or righted by the Divine in due time. You know them too, those sometimes painful course corrections. This may be the Camino's greatest solace—no hard choices to make except where you may eat or lay your head at night. The Camino offers those who walk it time to heal, to think or not to think at all, and to be comforted by its sleepy rhythms, one step at a time. Nothing is lost or wasted—all returning to God. Perhaps there is no magic in the Camino, since all of life moves us forward in this way. I myself feel the synchronicities and the turn of the wheel of my life more keenly as I walk the Way. Perhaps in this, for me, the Camino holds its greatest mystery of all.

By morning, we are heading by bus to the Basque seaside town of Biarritz on the Bay of Biscay. It is a twenty-minute ride, depending on how many times the bus stops for the locals. Today, it stops often. Luckily, it is fairly easy to locate the tourist bureau once here, and we are now headed for the beach. This fashionable seaside resort sits on the shoreline—with white houses and a castle or two perched on the cliffs above it. We have found the

Casino de Biarritz, right on the ocean, and walk through it down to the sand and to the promenade. It is easy to see why Biarritz has been a destination for royalty through the ages, as well as for bathers, surfers, and even whalers in bygone days. The warm breeze and the sea mist wrap us in their soothing, healing embrace. It is fairly intoxicating. The waves are frothing and lashing the rocks just below us. I have been told before to "go to the seashore" for those negative ions. Some of you may say it is voodoo science. I say it refreshes and balances mind, body, and soul—specifically *mine*.

Soon, we reach the Marian shrine of Notre Dame du Rocher (Our Lady of the Rock). She is the seaside sentinel and the keeper of the faith. This lovely white statue of Mary, sparkling iridescent in the sunshine, sits high atop a jutting rock formation which forms an archway. We cross under it and continue our walk. We then later explore the upper reaches of the town and sit for a while in the beautiful Church of Saint Martin. By early evening, we are enjoying *les fruits de mer et le vin rouge* (a seafood buffet and wine) at the casino restaurant. The bus makes regular trips back and forth to Bayonne, and we hop on one without much wait after dinner, both of us sorry it is time to leave. I find myself snuggled in my bed before I know it. Time has just whizzed by. My head is reeling from our adventures this day and this year, on and off the Camino. The last thing I remember as I drift off to sleep *ce soir* is the soft rain gently pelting the hotel windows.

By early light, we are heading on the TGV back to Paris and to the Hilton. We will have another full day in Paris tomorrow. But upon awaking the next morning, heavy rain is finally dampening our spirits. We opt to hang out at the hotel, simply to rest and relax before our flight home tomorrow. It is a good choice.

IV.
Summer 2014
Saint-Jean-Pied-de-Port to Burgos

175 MILES—15 DAYS

St. Jean-Pied-de-Port, Refuge Orisson, Roncesvalles, Zubiri,
Trinidad de Arre, Zariquiequi, Cirauqui, Villamayor, Torres del Rio,
Logrono, Nájera, Santo Domingo, Belorado, Villafranca Montes de
Oca, Atapuerca, Burgos

The Lord will perfect that which concerneth me. —Psalms 138: 8

I must confess, I have cheated again and booked a gîte d'étape for us in Saint-Jean-Pied-de-Port off the internet before I left home. I have also reserved two seats on the TGV—the speed train from Paris down to Bayonne. It is mid-summer the peak season for those walking the Camino, as well as for those on holiday. Oh me of little faith. I am not allowing the Camino to choose our beds tonight, as we start out. After all, Mother always said, "The Lord helps those who help themselves."

We have flown into the Paris Charles de Gaul Airport again. Jet-lagged and bleary-eyed, having flown all night, I am asking for help in just how to get to the train station, "*Bonjour, Madame! Comment allez-vous? Où est la gare, s'il vous plaît!*" Of course, the woman behind the information desk, thinking I must speak French well, gives us the directions in rapid French. She could have been speaking pig Latin for all I know. It all went over my head so fast that she may as well have been on speed dial. "*Parlez-vous anglais?*" I manage next. And with that, we have our directions in English and are heading for the train station, which is adjacent to the airport, to catch our train—but not before making a beeline over to the station patisserie for two éclairs au chocolat. Honestly, I don't eat like this at home (I know, I keep saying that). But, that heavenly aroma of fresh pastries wafting through the terminal has lured us in. Those sweet temptresses! No, I don't mean "temptations" although that word would do too.

Not soon enough, we are disembarking at la gare in beautiful Saint-Jean-Pied-de-Port. Our backs and shoulders and feet are adjusting to their new loads: "Oh no, *you* again." Of course, our backpacks and hiking poles are coming too. Last winter, just before Christmas, I fell and broke my wrist badly in several places and had to have surgery. I am grateful to have recovered fully, especially having bounced back (but more slowly) from a bout of adrenal fatigue and bronchitis due to the surgery—not to mention the stress at work. To say that I am glad to be back on the Camino again is an understatement. Marcia and I are excited to be together as well.

There is comfort in the familiarity of the train station and the town as we make our way over to our gîte. It is situated right on Rue de la Citadelle, the main pilgrim route through the town. We see it is closed until four o'clock. I am sure, preparing for the next round of pilgrims. Now, I am glad we have booked spaces for tonight. We hurry up the cobbled street to check in at the pilgrim welcome center—Accueil Pèlerin, staffed by the Association des Amis de Saint-Jacques. They are the clearing house for all information concerning pilgrims. They will know, most importantly, the state of the trails leaving Saint-Jean, as well as the weather conditions for tomorrow's hike through the

Pyrenees. Although it is summertime, the high mountain passes can still pose a problem. Neither of us wants to careen off the mountaintop in fog or in ice and snow. We also will need to decide whether to take the high road or the lower road across the mountains. It must be an informed decision. Marcia and I are already arguing about which route to take, she being the anxious one and I being the *fool,* who would indeed jump from that precipice. The Buddha taught "the middle way"—everything in moderation. *Peut-être* we will moderate each other in this, perhaps. No matter—I have a sneaky suspicion the Camino itself will have the final say.

There are two routes across the Pyrenees to Roncevaux (Roncesvalles in Spanish): the Valcarlos Route (the lower route by the river) or the Route Napoléon (the high route along the old Roman road). It is a little over sixteen miles either way. Our guidebook warns us to take the low road if it is windy already in Saint-Jean because we could otherwise meet with gale force winds and treacherous weather on the higher level route. Optimistically, I have booked ahead at the Refuge-Auberge d'Orisson (which is about five miles straight up on the high route) at the suggestion of a friend in Santa Fe who stayed there on his own foray across the mountains. I try to pay attention to guidance when it comes my way. And yes, we now have the green light from the pilgrim center to take the Napoleon Route starting early tomorrow morning. The winds are smiling, and the weather is holding up.

We are now free to re-explore Saint-Jean. This is the capital of the Basque province of Basse Navarre. The shops are full of local and regional products: wooly sheep toys for children, pottery and linens decorated in red peppers, brightly colored Spanish woven sandals (espadrilles). What is a pilgrim girl to do? Of course, we purchase nothing. By early evening, we have located a market nearby and have stocked up on our pèlerine supplies. Our gîte has opened too. We drop our packs by our little beds and walk over to Chez Edouard, hoping to have another wonderful cold calamari salad. It is not to be, for he has closed this evening early for a family event. So, we opt for pizza elsewhere, stop back in at the Église Notre Dame, and then head back to our gîte early. As the sun sets, it is turning ominously cool.

This morning, the sun is barely peeking over the misty blue mountains, and we are already downstairs having café au lait and toasted baguettes. We are anxious to get up the steep part of the mountain before the heat of the day—if there *is* any heat, that is. It is a chilly morning, and the fog lies low against the hills. Other pilgrims are leaving early too. The cobbled street just outside our gîte is bustling with activity and anticipation. We make our way down the Rue de la Citadelle through the old Porte d'Espagne and cross the bridge over the River Nive. I am sad to leave Saint-Jean, knowing I may never pass this way again. We are now walking up Rue d'Espagne, and we must set our sights for Spain. At a junction, we come upon a cluster of bright yellow signs in French and in the Basque language that point us right and then a quick left onto Route Napoléan. It is a black-tarred, narrow road that ascends steeply and doesn't let up for almost five miles. It is slow going.

Eventually we reach our destination—the Auberge Orisson. This is another time I am glad we booked ahead. We arrive early afternoon, rather exhausted, and once again lots of fellow pilgrims are also coming in. The gîte is full. It seems our bunk beds have been awaiting our arrival. At dinner, we are served a four-course pilgrim meal, all of us seated around long wooden tables in the bar. The sky glows yellow and orange against thick purple clouds as the sun sets over the mountains. And, as lightning streaks across the dark sky and thunder fills the air, the sky opens up a torrent of rain. I get the feeling the rains come often here; after all, we are bedded down this night in the midst of the clouds themselves. Tucked in, I wonder what awaits us tomorrow as we press on, and I also think about this ancient path and what history it may yield.

This is Napolean's route across the Pyrenees, of course, but the history here runs even deeper. We are approaching the Roncevaux Pass at Saragossa, where Charlemagne's army was turned back in 778 and his rear guard soundly defeated. Charlemagne, King of the Franks and the first recognized Holy Roman Emperor, was battling the Saracens (the Moors) into Spain in this region in the eighth century, in the early Middle Ages. Charlemagne's rear guard was attacked by the Basques as his army was returning to France from their battles with the Moors. The story goes that Roland, Charlemagne's nephew and his vassal, proudly refused to sound his olifant (a hunting horn) for reinforcements and so was killed along with the paladins, his fabled twelve peers. Later, the famous Song of Roland sprang forth, the French epic poem of the massacre. It was an early tale that ushered in the era of knights and chivalry in the Middle Ages. My head is spinning now as the rain lulls me into deep sleep.

By early morning, the blue of the sky is barely peeking out of the low clouds and fog. As we walk, a rainbow glistens in the mist over the rolling mountains. It is the promise of a clear day ahead. We see shepherd paths that look like ribbons winding through the green of the hills below us. We are literally walking in the clouds. Spotted mares and their folds graze just off the pavement nearby. Only now, I see that one certain little spotted pony has gotten his tail caught in the crevice between two large rocks. I quickly drop my backpack and start towards him. Meanwhile, the mare heads for me, protecting her baby. Then, they both suddenly turn and run off. I am the fool left holding the bag (literally) since I have now picked up my pack and am trudging up the path once again. Yes, that baby horse was merely scratching his hind quarters on the rocks. Go ahead and laugh at me, I don't care. I am laughing too, at myself and my own naiveté. I am a city girl. What can I say?

We are now walking through a vast undulating landscape of hills and then down into grassy tracks and woods. A simple marker made of stone three miles later announces our passage into Spain. *Au revoir la France! Hola España!* You have to know my favorite phrase in Spanish: *"No hablo Español!"* (I don't speak Spanish!) Why confuse my bare French with Spanish lessons, I have reasoned. We have over four hundred-and-fifty miles to get through Spain to Santiago de Compostela like this. Nevertheless, we are excited to have crossed into Spain, and we walk on until we reach Col Lepoeder (at about 5,000 feet). Here, our walking guide tells us to look for the first view of rooftops of the Abbey at Roncesvalles. But, somehow, they have escaped us. We eventually get to a clearing by a chapel that in times past was dedicated to Roland (Roldan in Spanish). The chapel is closed, so we head left down the roadway into what we believe is town. We end up doubling back to make sure we enter Roncesvalles on the Camino by the Abbey. I get cross when I have to retrace my steps since every step matters. By now, it is late afternoon and starting to drizzle cold rain. Eventually, we reach the Abbey. It sits at the bottom of a long, steep, muddy footpath through the woods. We have gotten here just in time and just as it begins to pour. Thunder rumbles in the distance.

We drop our bags and poles and dripping plastic ponchos just inside the entryway at a large stone refugio. This refugio was once a hospital for *peregrinos* (Spanish for pilgrims) built in the early part of the twelfth century. We have read that it is run by the monastery here and staffed by ex-pilgrim volunteers. And so it is, smiling English speakers greet us and check us in. We have to show our passports, get our pilgrim credentials stamped, and pay a modest fee in order to get a bed (standard procedure all places). There is a long line to register, but, fortunately, we are assigned bunk beds and are directed up a long flight of stairs to our dormitory room. For another small fee, we can get our clothes washed and dried. Now that's luxury! Here we meet several young women from the States who are walking the Camino on their summer breaks from college. They are sweet, and nobody minds the generation gap.

Early evening, we walk down the slippery cobbled street, dodging the rain, first to the church, with its beautiful stained glass windows, and then to a restaurant. The place is packed. They are serving a pilgrim meal en masse: a hearty dinner of fish or chicken, pasta, vegetables, soup, flan, crusty bread, and *vino tinto* (red wine). *Salud!*

Today, the rain has stopped. We are walking in fog through Roncesvalles to a *panaderia* for *café con leche y pan* (coffee with milk and bread). Then, just leaving the town, we stock up on supplies at a *supermercado* which obviously thrives on the pilgrim trade: peanuts, more bananas, toilet paper. Did I say toilet paper? Oh yes, we have actually been reduced to hoarding it by now—it can be so scarce in some of the refugios. Both of us have wads of toilet paper stuffed in our pockets. We are little refined hobos. It is the seedier side of the pilgrimage that no one wants to talk about. Oh, and I am not supposed to say that we all have to take an occasional *potty break* (Marcia's term, not mine) in the woods too. Oops!

We are heading for the village of Zubiri. It is fourteen miles from Roncesvalles in the Basque province of Navarra. The walk is exceedingly beautiful and shady through rural areas and several small hamlets. By the end of the day, we cross a medieval bridge over the Rio Arga to enter Zubiri. The folklore surrounding this bridge, popularly known as the "rabies bridge," is that walking your dog back and forth over the bridge cures it of rabies. Alrighty, then! Just how can anyone walk a rabid dog anywhere? I think too much sometimes.

This is a beautiful little village nestled in the river valley, with its whitewashed, timbered Basque-style houses. Pots of

Alto del Perdón

bright red geraniums decorate the balconies and window sills everywhere. We inquire at a local bar for a good refugio for the night and are directed just down the street to the Albergue Zubiri. Once again, we are fortunate to reserve two bunk beds, a pilgrim meal, and a mini-breakfast. We get the last two beds. This evening we sit for a lovely dinner with several Spanish women who are on holiday and are walking a portion of the Camino together. One or two of them speak some English. We laugh and raise our glasses of red wine to toast our impromptu party of peregrinos. *"Buen Camino!"*

We are hoping to get to Trinidad de Arre today, which is almost eleven miles away. To regain the Camino, we have to backtrack over the bridge and then turn right up a steep wooded path to climb out of the river valley. Looking back, the view of Zubiri below is breathtaking. Looking forward, we carry on uphill and down again, through dense woods and then fields and by farm houses passing through several more hamlets. We stop for awhile at a refugio and bar where fellow pilgrims are congregated outside on the patio having coffee and mid-morning snacks. A large, modern, iron sculpture of a pilgrim out front welcomes us real ones. Refreshed, we walk up a narrow, tarred road lined with grasses and poppies until we eventually reach the village of Zabaldica and the Church of Saint Stephen.

A kindly nun stands at the door to greet us, along with a black and white cat who has come running over—cats know. Of course, I dig a tin of cat food out of my bag and feed kitty before we go into the church—this lovely, lovely Church of St. Stephen. We are struck by a figure of Jesus on the cross as we enter. A sea of green post-it notes surround him. Peregrinos have left all manner of prayers and notes here. I add my own, as well as the prayers I have carried from home from my Carmelite friends. Marcia and I sit for a time on one of the benches and take in the beautiful Spanish *retablo* (altarpiece) of renderings of Jesus, Mary, and various saints, including St. James. Kitty joins us, purring, and climbs into Marcia's lap for a short siesta. After awhile, we climb the spiral stone stairs to the bell tower and ring the church bell. It tolls its melodic ding and dong across the valley. As we leave, we see that the nuns maintain an *albergue* just next door to the church. We cannot stay. It is too early in our day, and we must press on.

After more than an hour of walking, we cross another medieval bridge into the village of Trinidad de Arre. Immediately after the bridge, we have arrived at our resting place for the night, the Basilica de la Sanctisima Trinidad and its refugio. This refugio was once a pilgrim hospital. We are hoping to find beds here, and we do. A *padre* stamps our credentials, takes our euros, and shows us upstairs to a large dormitory room full of bright blue bunk beds. He has assigned us to two bunk beds in a small side room with all female pilgrims. *Muchas gracias, Senor!* "All that *snorking* going on!" groaned one of our new French friends one morning a few days ago. Our friend was rolling her eyes and scowling dramatically. Of course, she was trying to say *"snoring,"* but we decided we liked her word for it much better. "Ha, ha, ha—snorking!" Now, we have just increased our chances of a decent night's sleep away from all those—well, snorkers in the main dormitory.

After sorting out our things, we visit the chapel and then sit for awhile in the sunshine in the enclosed grassy courtyard. We eat something small at a local restaurant, find an open mercado for tomorrow's supplies, and then return early for bed. I am tossing and turning until I too let out my own little snork and fall fast asleep.

Pamplona, the capital of Navarre and a large fortress town, is on our radar today. It is almost four miles away. We want to get through Pamplona, however, and walk as far as we can, weather and feet permitting. A British woman in our room last night was doctoring a huge blister on the sole of one of her feet; we are fortunate not to have such troubles ourselves. We are actually walking through the suburbs of Pamplona from the time we leave Trinidad de Arre in long stretches of a commercial district with its apartments and shops and increasing dirt and traffic. We eventually cross an old pilgrim bridge, the Puente de los Peregrinos, into the walled city. Little did we know we are in Pamplona during the two-week festival of San Firmin and the running of the bulls. Thankfully, we are walking through the city central just after the big party and after the bulls have run. A few stragglers are walking the streets, but mostly it is all over. The streets are littered with trash, and maintenance workers are out in force trying to clean it all up. I realize this is a national Spanish tradition, this running of the bulls and the bull fights, but how much longer must these poor animals endure man's inhumanity? I have read that many, even in Spain, are advocating change. We can see that Pamplona has much to offer, otherwise, but the cathedral is closed now, so we walk on. It takes us quite a long time to walk through Pamplona and emerge on the other side. By the way, Saint Firmin was an early bishop and martyr in the ancient kingdom of Navarre. He met his death being dragged through the streets by angry bulls.

We are noticing that many of the churches we are passing, especially those in small villages, are closed. Maybe it's the number of pilgrims walking the Camino these days through Spain and the burden it must present for the local communities—I don't know. Or, it could be that the shops and churches close up in the scorching heat of the day for Spain's famed siesta.

As we leave Pamplona, we climb a winding, narrow dirt path steadily up and out of the valley. We are in the midst of wheat fields that look parched by the sun. But the sky is gray, and rain is approaching. This might be a good thing for the fields, but it is not so good for us right now. As we round a bend, a great expanse of sunflowers stretching to the horizon awaits us. Bright yellow sunflowers stand majestically in the fields, their faces tilted expectantly toward the heavens. We both snap pictures quickly. It is time for us to find shelter; we have walked over ten miles today. We continue to climb and eventually reach the Basque village of Zariguiegui and the Posada Ardogi Albergue. This is another lovely refuge. We unpack and return downstairs to their small but cozy restaurant and bar and have hot soup, bread with olive oil, and a glass of vino tinto. The rain begins just as we climb the stairs again and say *"buenas noches"*—good night.

This morning, we continue climbing uphill. Windmills are perched on a ridge in the distance. They get closer and closer until we can almost reach out and touch them. We are at the Alto del Perdón, the hill of forgiveness. The view below is breathtakingly beautiful. Hamlets dot the landscape along with checkered patterns of farmland and fields. A line of life-size, dark, metal sculptures stretches across the hilltop where we are standing. It is a caravan of pilgrims on mules and on horseback—some walking too. Their long staffs steady their way. A dog follows along behind. It is a touching memorial to the Camino and to those who travel the path of the twinkling stars. We can add our names to that certain band of wanderers who have walked this path before us just beneath the Milky Way. We wander, but we are not lost.

Our narrow way down is steep and rocky; we go slowly. We come upon an iron cross with a scallop shell. This cross, draped in ribbons and flowers, marks the place where a pilgrim died trying to get to Santiago de Compostela. We walk on through several small villages and then reach the town of Obanos. We have come about seven miles. We are weighing our options now. Our book recommends a less than two-mile detour from here to the twelfth-century church at Eunate where early pilgrims were buried. We can see the road is flat before us through grassy fields, so we head toward Eunate. Before long, we come upon a friendly young Spanish woman who is walking five happy little dogs on leashes. She is definitely doing her part. We pet them for a while, dog therapy, and walk on.

The Iglesia de Santa Maria at Eunate is a beautiful octagonal Romanesque church set out in the countryside. We are glad we diverted here and are also fortunate the church is open. Inside, we find a very interesting statue of Mary and the Christ Child. She wears a gold crown. A vase of bright pink and red gladiolas has been placed in front of her. The windows all around are tall and narrow and barely let in the light. There is an air of mystery and reverence here. Outside again, we are told by a young Spanish woman, in faltering English, that the local custom is to pray and walk seven times backwards around the church within its iron fence. I am not sure where this rather superstitious, quirky custom came from, but, okay, we can do this. It is a practice in mindfulness, if nothing else, much like walking a labyrinth. After which, we stop by a small pilgrim center next door run by the nuns and get our pilgrim credentials stamped. It is getting hot, and we have farther to go.

It takes us longer to regain the Camino than expected, but we are soon enough walking the cobbled streets in the large town of Puente la Reina. The Church of Santiago here is open. There is a beautiful gold statue of St. James on one wall. Rows of glowing white votives have been placed at his feet. The interior of this church is cool and serene, the perfect place for us to rest our feet for just a minute before we press on.

Leaving Puente la Reina, we cross an old pilgrim bridge over the Arga River. Then we walk quite a while by a busy highway. Our dirt path is separated from the road by an unsightly metal fence. Creative peregrinos have taken up the challenge, however, to make this segment sacred: hundreds of twig crosses have been stuck in the chain fencing. Marcia and I both are amazed at its striking, primitive beauty. You just can't make up something like this.

As we approach the village of Cirauqui, I pointedly take my pen in hand and scrawl in the margins of our guidebook "the beautiful village on the hill." Indeed, the hillside town of Cirauqui, coming up in front of us, fairly sparkles like a diamond in the late afternoon sunshine. We see as we get there that the town itself is an intricate maze of buildings. But, the waymarks for the Camino are our steady guide. The red and white markers of the Le Puy Route have long given way to blue signs with a yellow star. The tail of the star points west in the direction of Santiago de Compostela. Arrays of pink and red geraniums spill out of window boxes everywhere we look. Scallop shells, gourds, and sweet images of Jesus and of St. James are mounted around doors and windows.

We walk through this lovely town first, to orient ourselves, and then double back to a refugio just across from the church to inquire as to beds. The proprietor is sitting across the street, on a bench in front of the church, smoking a cigarette. She watched us pass by the first time, and now that we have returned, she is smiling. She knows this is the best refugio and the only refugio in town. Lucky us! We are able to book both bunk beds and dinner here. Fellow pilgrims are already converging. The place is bustling with activity as well as inactivity. Several pilgrims are stretched out on their beds relaxing and napping. Racks of laundry are drying on the balcony in the sun. Chatter and excitement run high. This is a busy place. There was no time for us to waiver about where to stay lest we find ourselves camped outside for the night. No, no—that was not an option at all. If the truth be told, Marcia had been reluctant to stay here initially, so we had walked on. But the Camino wasn't having any of it—no fickle Ms. Fancy this night.

We claim our beds, shower, and add our own wet laundry to the racks on the balcony. And then we walk across to the Gothic church of San Roman—this one is open. I would not have wanted to miss it. This is another beautiful old restored church on the Camino. The altar is emblazoned in gold and red. There are two different images of Mary and the Ascension. In both, she is surrounded by cherubs. It occurs to me that these old sanctuaries are the true refugios on the Way. We sit for a long while.

By dinner, we find ourselves seated in a cozy, dimly lit dining room just below the refugio. It looks like a dungeon, though, it was most likely a cellar at one time. The walls are made of river rock and other stone. As it turns out, the chef is the husband of the woman who checked us in. We are served, family style, a huge platter of tasty *pasta con salsa de carne*, salade nicoise, a basket of crusty bread, vino tinto, and flan. We could not have had a better pilgrim meal anywhere, and their hospitality is friendly and open-hearted. We finally drag ourselves exhausted up to our little beds. I happen to like humility—it suits me.

This morning, we get surprisingly good café con leche from a vending machine downstairs and then head out early. Other peregrinos, of course, have the same idea, and we are all milling around in a sort of traffic jam—Camino style. It is a beautiful day; the air is crisp and cool. We wind our way out of the village and eventually cross an old Roman bridge over the River Salado. Beware this river. Probably the earliest pilgrim guide was written in Latin in the twelfth century by, it is believed, one Aimery Picaud, a cleric from Poitou, in France. He warned travelers that there were those sitting on the banks of this river just waiting to flay the poor, unwitting horse that drank from its waters. Those men knew full well that death from drinking the bad water would soon follow. I look quickly to the banks of the river, right and then left, and hurry on.

About four miles later, we reach the town of Lorca and stop at a bar there for a break. Taking up our packs and poles again, we walk by the Church of San Salvador.

We can see the church is open. Marcia refuses to walk up the long stairway. She has "put her foot down" and will not budge. As for me, I can't seem to help myself and climb what could be fifty stairs and go in. I am glad I do. The church is beautiful with an image of Saint James mounted on the wall. But what I enjoy the most is the Gothic cloisters, with a rose garden, that is next to the church. It is a paradise of red and coral roses and tall pines—a grassy, peaceful place. Marcia waits on the street, having no choice unless she wants to walk on without me. She does not.

Past the towns of Villatuerta and then Estella, I am disappointed to find that the monastery at Irache is closed. But, what sits across the road from the monastery is rather delightful—a *fuente del vino*. Yes, a wine fountain. The Bodegas Irache offers free red wine and water to the pilgrims, from two spigots, with an invitation to drink their fine wine and raise our glasses to happiness. Only in Spain! The Camino is literally serving up red wine. I am certainly happy now, for we have deposited our backpacks by the wrought iron fence and are sitting on the curb enjoying our wine. After a few sips, however, this wine that is meant to spur us on, is having the opposite effect on me. All I want to do is stretch out in the grass and take a long snooze on this lazy, hot summer's afternoon. We must walk on. The sun is blazing overhead, but we are walking on a relatively flat dirt path by fields and vineyards. We had read that this area of Spain in Navarre is renowned for its vineyards and for its very good vino tinto, both of which I can now attest to personally.

We have walked fifteen miles today and are looking for beds in the small village of Villamayor de Monjardin, but the first refugio we find is full. We are fortunate to get the last two beds in the only other one, which is up the street. It is slim pickings. We end up in a little private room on the top floor. Later in the evening, we agree to share our space with another pilgrim, a very nice woman from Hungary who speaks some English. She is a teacher there and has managed to save her money to make this pilgrimage. We are all grateful to have a bed this night at all. Pilgrims are being turned away. Did I say that the shower is tepid and the toilets are loud and leaky? Marcia is the brave one and comes back to break the news. "Never mind—no shower for me tonight!" I laugh with a groan. I am too tired to care. We do find bar food next door for an early dinner and then turn in.

We are at the same bar again by early morning, having our coffee and toast. We have read that the path ahead is relatively easy and flat, but that it has little shade. This proves to be true. We go through two more villages and, after twelve miles or so, stop for the night at an alberge in Torres del Rio. The restaurant and bar is downstairs, and the refugio is just above on the second floor. This is a popular place. Locals are there eating and passing the time under umbrellas at outside tables—always a good sign. For eighteen euros (roughly twenty dollars), we reserve two bunk beds, dinner, and our small customary pilgrim breakfast. I have written in the margins of our book "great place." It is friendly and clean and rather charming. We locate a small mercado and buy supplies for tomorrow's peregrino picnic lunch on the road: bananas, peanuts, yogurt and then walk to the old church. Unfortunately, it is closed until later. Only later, we are you-know-where doing you-know-what—in our beds plotting our distance for the next day.

Today, the Camino takes us uphill and then down again through valleys and around sharp curves. We pass through an area of pilgrim rock piles. Yes, pilgrims have left cairns, little towers of small stones, here as if to say, "I passed this way on the Camino along with those before me!" Some pebbles are neatly arranged to spell out in English: "Live, love, and let go!" That "let go" part seems the hardest for me. And today, I am clinging to the particularly wistful question of whether I will be transformed at all by the Camino. Maybe it comes, and we are the last to know. We pass through more rows of grapevines. Pink and yellow rosebushes have been lovingly cultivated at the edge of the vineyards right by our path. It is all so beautiful.

Almost seven miles along, we have come to the town of Viana with its narrow cobbled streets. Bright red posies are draped over iron railings on balconies everywhere we look. From here, we are afforded our first view of Logroño, off in the distance. We are moving into the Basque region of La Rioja, which is perhaps the best known wine-producing region in Spain. Logrono is its capital. Our path takes us by an outlying commercial area and factory and then through woods and across a footbridge over a river. We then cross through a tunnel; we can hear cars zipping by on the road overhead. Marcia poses for a picture, smiling. She is standing by a huge scallop shell painted aqua on the cement wall leaving the tunnel. It reads *"Buen Camino!"*

The sun is blazing. We are walking down a flat, dry, dusty road for miles until we come upon an oasis. An enterprising man has parked his red van by the roadside—its doors are flung wide open. He is seated on a folding chair under an umbrella, offering fruit and water and all manner of trinkets—crosses and shells—to those who walk by. For a donation, of course. An accommodating pair of young British guys are out with their cameras and other film equipment interviewing and photographing him and generally, capturing the moment. They are doing a documentary on the Camino, they tell us. He is only too happy to oblige them. I notice they have no car nearby. They are walking the Camino too, only they are also lugging along their heavy equipment. *"Buenos dias, Senor,"* I manage. The man flashes a big smile as we buy two bottles of water. I ask him if we could feed his dog who is tied up on a long leash and lying in the shade of the van. *"Si, Senoras! Si!"* Where upon, I drag out dog food from Marcia's pack and place it under the van with some water, as that little dog wags his tail in happy approval. It is not that this dog needs our help, really. We just like doing it—just for grins. That friend in Santa Fe would be smirking disapprovingly right about now.

We are walking by a string of small houses soon enough that I assume must be on the outskirts of Logroño. More folks are sitting under umbrellas and under the trees in their front yards hawking peregrino patches and shells. Several dogs are tied up and standing on their doghouses right by the road, excited to meet and greet. I buy a patch (a white shell with a red cross on it) to add to my collection, which by now trails down the back of my backpack. Still shopping, are you? Well, I am not dead yet. What I *am* right now, however, is exhausted. And, my feet hurt. We are finally walking into the large town of Logroño in the nick of time; we have walked twelve miles this hot day. We have come to the Puente de Piedra, the long bridge over the Río Ebro, and turn left to cross it and enter Logroño.

The large municipal hostel at Logroño looks jam-packed. Pilgrims are congregated outside and are also literally spilling out of the windows. We decide it is too busy for us and walk on. Just two blocks further up the street, we find an attractive, white-washed hotel. We inquire at the desk. They maintain an albergue portion of the hotel for pilgrims. We quickly book two bunk beds and settle right in. I pull off my hiking boots and stretch out on my little bed with its bright blue plastic sheet. No worries—my feet are propped up singing a silent song of joy.

Refugios and albergues will provide a pillowcase and bottom sheet of some kind, but that is it. They are trying to cut down on their costs, but more importantly, they are trying to prevent BEDBUGS. Yes, that's right—those pesky little traveling companions we have heard so much about since we began our journey. We have seen a few pilgrims spraying their beds obsessively before they put down their sleeping bags. Ironically, those are the ones most likely to get them, I think—those who are fussing around and focused on them. So far, we have had no problems. Nonetheless, I have carefully laid out my sleeping bag shell, which I use as a top and bottom sheet. You may remember, we sent our sleeping bags home long ago.

By early evening, we are out exploring the city and walking its broad central promenade. The streets are full of people enjoying the warmth of a summer night. We stop in the Church of Santiago. A statue of St. James is at the altar. There are also two beautiful statues of Mary, one in gold in which she is shown trampling the dragon. We dine outside and return for a good night's sleep. As I drift off, I think about what Mother used to say when we were children: "Sleep tight, and don't let the bedbugs bite."

We are walking in another commercial district and by gas stations as we leave Logroño this morning. We are planning to reach Nájera today. We will have walked seventeen miles. We reach the Pantano de la Grajera (a reservoir), and it takes us quite a long while to walk around it. But we are also in woods and shade—no complaints. Past the reservoir, we are walking down a pleasant dirt road by vineyards and then eventually into the town of Navarette. The interior of the church at Navarette is crowned in Baroque gold, with several exquisite renderings of Mary and the Christ Child. The altar is filled with vases of pink gladiolas, red roses, white mums, and lilies. It is quite beautiful. The sweet fragrance of flowers, candles, and incense fills the air. We rest here and then continue down the Camino.

On the outskirts of Navarette, we walk past a dilapidated set of empty buildings behind a fence on our left. Someone keeps several dogs in a dark pen on the edge of the property as watch dogs. They are barking wildly and running back and forth in a cramped covered space of about four feet by two feet. I can tell from a distance that they are skinny and unkempt—it is painful to see. So now let me complain. We have noticed a rather callous disregard for the farm dogs, especially in Spain. They are tied up to guard abandoned property, usually isolated and out in the middle of nowhere. The sad faces of these dogs say it all. With water bowls always empty and often with no shade, they don't even look up as we walk by and greet them. I realize that I can't do anything about it. I simply pray for them to find kindness and better circumstances somehow and then walk on. It is painful for Marcia too. I wish I understood planet earth better. I will say, I prefer walking in the real world to an illusion or delusion, however painful the world may seem sometimes. A very astute friend of mine (who was a social worker and family counselor) used to say, "It is better to *know* than not to know." Yes, I climbed down out of my ivory tower long ago. And, what is reality and what is illusion, anyway? According to the sage, it is all illusion. Perhaps true wisdom sees the suffering of others and works to change it, but then in the end shifts its focus to the beauty in this world and to the peace that passes all understanding—I don't know. You can see I haven't gotten there yet. And waxing philosophical doesn't make me feel much better, either, as I continue to think about those dogs all the way up the path.

Just past the Alto de San Antón Pass, we drop down into woods and then a valley of more vineyards and cairns. Cairns, those little stacked monuments of rocks, are everywhere. Some of the cairns have been placed under the watchful eye of an old tree—its wide branches dipping down low, almost caressing them. We place our own simple heap of stones here and then sit in the welcome shade of this lovely tree.

Walking on, we are catapulted back in time once more as we approach the Poyo Roldán (Roland's Hill). Here, it is said, Charlemagne's knight, Roland, waged a fierce battle against the Syrian giant Ferragut and won. A sign in Spanish and English marks the spot. A primitive, round stone hut stands high on the hill, most likely also in commemoration of the event.

We are now walking into the commercial outlying area of Nájera. A poem written in Castilian and translated into German has been painted on the wall of a factory we are passing by. Our guidebook graciously translates it into English. It is something about just what motivates pilgrims to walk the Camino. The conclusion, in a roundabout way, is that only God knows. I find some comfort in this, since my best thinking yields no better answer as to just why I personally am drawn here too.

We are excited to get to Nájera and even more excited to find a cozy refugio just as we cross the bridge over the Río

Leafy Tunnel of Time

Najerilla and enter the old part of town. It is the Puerta de Nájera Alberque de Peregrinos, a charming place that offers bunk beds for only ten euros. The *Señora* who checks us in is friendly and helpful. She directs us to put our hiking boots on a tall shelf among the others in the hallway. Those mud-caked, dirty, dusty boots all lined up in a row have stories to tell, if we will but sit and listen. They whisper tales of hopes and dreams. They speak of blisters and sore feet and joy and triumph, too. We place our boots at the end of one row. They have their own secrets to tell. "Be easy on us," I tell them. "We are all doing the best we can." Ssssssh—just listen.

By sunrise this morning, we are already out having café con leche y pan at a restaurant by the river. We then gather our packs and poles and stride down the narrow cobbled streets heading out of beautiful Nájera. Shopkeepers are just beginning to open their doors. We have about thirteen miles to go today to get to the large town of Santo Domingo de la Calzada. We mainly walk along a dirt road through fields and vineyards and then by a long stretch of golden wheat fields parched by the sun. They stretch as far as the eye can see against the horizon. Clusters of bright red poppies dot the landscape along both sides of the road. The vastness of this area is astounding. Birds soar and then ride the wind; they glisten in the early morning sunlight.

Marcia and I are both tired today, and as the sun beats down mercilessly about noon, we stop for a picnic lunch in a small village. Down the road again, a mile or two later, Marcia notices that she has left her hat way behind somewhere—this her aqua hat, at that. Maybe it blew off her head in the wind when she was taking pictures of sunflowers on the side of the road. Whatever, it is missing. Not a good thing in the gathering heat. But we are not going back to look for it on some wild goose chase. Just as she stops her fretting, we turn around to see her bright agua hat in the distance moving steadily towards us. A good Samaritan peregrino has just happened to spot it and is bringing it along. Marcia bursts out into whoops of joy—she is so relieved. She thanks this thoughtful man profusely. I am reminded of a story my minister told one Sunday years ago that I have never forgotten. She had lost something at home and spent over an hour ransacking her drawers and searching high and low for it, with no results. Finally, she gave up and just sat down, only to gaze across her study and see the object sitting on her bookshelf in plain view. Dr. Ann was teaching us about the spiritual principle of "divine inaction." Or, another way to put it, once you have done all you can, let go and let God. I smile to myself as Marcia's hat is handed over.

Reaching Santo Domingo, we have located the Monasterio de la Encarnación which we have read offers a refugio for peregrinos run by Cistercian nuns. It is a large, ancient stone facility. As we enter, a nun is sitting in a booth-like little office checking pilgrims in. Fortunately, Marcia and I are able to book two bunk beds. As we head up a long stone staircase to our dormitory room, we are met with a wall of boots already lined up on shelves. This place is filling up fast. We are assigned a room in which there are ten bunk beds. All of the beds are covered with red-and-blue checkered bedspreads. I snap a quick picture of Marcia sitting on her little lower bunk busily sorting her things for a shower.

We have also read the colorful story surrounding the seventh-century Cathedral of San Salvador which is located just up the street. But by the time we get there it is closing for the day, and that rooster and hen inside are bedding down for the night. Yes, I have managed to get Marcia (with her bird phobia) to the door of the Cathedral, but no further, particularly since she read the tale too. The story goes that certain parents and their son who were traveling the Camino found refuge for the night at an inn in town. The next morning, the innkeeper's daughter accused the son of theft—the young man having rejected her romantic advances. Alas, he was hanged. On their return from Santiago, the bereaved parents found their son still hanging but not yet dead. They immediately begged the judge to release him. Where upon, the judge bellowed out something like "Your son is as dead as what is on my dinner plate!" Well, you might have guessed the story from here. The fowl on his plate leaped up and flew away, and the young man was redeemed. Ever since, a rooster and hen have been kept in a cage hung high up in the cathedral to commemorate the miracle. I have read since that, for humane purposes, pairs of birds are rotated monthly in and out. Even still, if the truth be told, I too am glad the cathedral is closing right about now and that I don't have to go in and witness the spectacle for myself. Cock a doodle doo!

Belorado is our destination for today. It is almost fifteen miles away. We have passed through several pretty villages, but we keep walking. By the time we reach the town, we are exhausted, as usual. We are staying at the lovely Cuatro Cantones Albergue de Peregrinos. This is a pink refugio; its black iron railings on two levels are spilling over with bright red and coral geraniums. We are glad to be here. Later, we walk the narrow cobblestone streets to one of the old churches nearby. Storks have built large nests high at the top of its bell tower. They, the watchers, are perched in their nests or flying in and out of what I call "storklandia"! After we visit their beautiful church, we walk back. Only now, I am sniffling. It seems I am developing a cold. I have to hide it; no colds are allowed. I suspect I caught it from another hapless soul sick and coughing only a few beds away from me, a refugio or two ago. I have pulled out my over-the-counter cold medicine and my tissues. Every time I sneeze I say with a laugh, "Ha ha, allergies, you know!" in an effort to hide the sordid truth. I can't even tell Marcia for fear she will develop it too as some sort of sympathetic reaction.

By morning, I am feeling better. As we leave the village of Belorado, we walk past a huge colorful modern mural of St. James, the Peregrino, that has been painted on the side of a building. We continue down the Avenida Camino de Santiago out of town. The terrain is changing. We are entering the dense woods of the Montes de Oca and the region of Castille-Leon. The Camino is a veritable roller coaster ride now. We walk down a long, steep graveled trail and then up again. This goes on for several miles. I find it quite fascinating, the huge ascent and then deep dip into the basin of the hills. Thank God the path is well laid out. We are in the middle of nowhere, but going somewhere, I presume. Oh yes, we have set our sights for nearby Villafranca Montes de Oca. Seven miles of this terrain is quite enough for us today. But the long, steep descent is pushing my toes forward in my hiking boots, causing pressure and, after a while, soreness in my big toes. By the time we get to Villafranca, I see that both toenails are bruised. Of course, Marcia is having no problems with her boots or feet. (I wish this was just creative writing and me making this up, but oh no!) I may as well bid my big toenails *adios*. I know I will lose them, as I did when I ran a half-marathon years ago. Get a grip—it is only toenails. Although I have stuffed cotton balls all around my toes, it has been to no avail. I limp in pain into Villafranca.

But Marcia is about to upstage even me. We have booked beds at the refugio at the renovated grand old Hospital de San Antonio Abad. However, we check back out as fast as we checked in, much to the chagrin of the lady behind the desk. Why so? Well, a beautiful peacock happened to strut by in the courtyard as we were being shown our room. Marcia freaked out and refused to stay there any longer. "I understand, Marcia!" I tell her that, truly, if it were a serpent that happened by, it would be I who was exiting stage left. Today, the sister act has turned into a bad comedy. We trudge to the municipal refugio just down the street and are fortunate to find bunk beds in a very large dormitory room of pilgrims, both men and women. This refugio has a big kitchen. We cook ourselves our trusty menu of pasta marinara and share it with our pilgrim friend from Hungary who, it turns out, is also staying here. The day has ended in a sweet time with friends. By bedtime, I am fast asleep almost before I hit the pillow.

This morning, although my toenails are still rather bluish, they are not so sore. Sleep is a healing balm for most things. We are loaded up with water and other pilgrim supplies. Our book has warned us to start out early. We will walk for hours in dense woods through an unpopulated area before we reach San Juan de Ortega. We are both a little apprehensive as to what we might encounter in this mountainous, secluded section of the Camino; hopefully, not bandits. We have read that, in the Middle Ages, this area was notorious for attacks by bandits on hapless, unsuspecting pilgrims.

We are only too happy to reach the hamlet of San Juan de Ortega (literally, Saint John of the Nettles) after walking about eight miles through the forest. Thankfully, there were no bandits lurking in the woods—such extreme isolation can be a little unnerving. We stop for a visit at the beautifully-restored Romanesque Church of San Nicolas de Bari and the tomb of San Juan de Ortega. The church offers a cool dark haven from the sun for just a little while. Juan de Ortega, also known as Saint John the Hermit, set himself to restoring roads and building bridges along the Camino in this part of Spain. He also constructed a monastery and hospice attached to the church as a relief for the many pilgrims who had just descended from the isolated mountains. He practiced contemplation deep in the woods here, in a hermitage that he erected for himself. I would have liked this kindly man very much.

We press on. The passage is fairly level, and we are walking by fields on a dirt road, eventually into the village of Atapuerca.

We have come eleven miles for the day. We see the village nestled in the valley on the skyline. After exploring this small village quickly, we double back, both of us pondering our choices for the night. There are only two refugios. We are hot and tired and grouchy. Fellow pilgrims have already formed a line outside the door of one of the refugios, waiting for it to open. The other refugio is closed until much later. Take it or leave it. Fortunately, we are able to get beds. We walk down the street to a small, family-owned restaurant and bar for dinner. It offers a pilgrim meal. We both choose fish and chips and a salad. We return, knowing only too well that morning will come quickly. One of our friends, Jennifer, has arrived just as darkness approaches. She is the last to get a bed. We are all delighted to see each other. So, is divine inaction at play, or shall we call it synchronicity, or chance, or a happy coincidence? I dare not assign too much meaning, since I will never know anyway. Maybe it just doesn't matter.

As we leave the village this morning, we turn left up a steep hill into more woods. The birds are chirping and cheering us on. Descending, we pass a huge labyrinth that has been laid out on the plateau by fellow pilgrims. I am amused—as though the Camino itself isn't already a labyrinth-like puzzle. The truth is we are all trying to find meaning in the experience of the Camino, and certainly in this journey called life. The labyrinth is lovely nonetheless. It stretches out across the wet grass amid the soft mist of early morning.

We are heading for Burgos, the last leg on our pilgrimage for this year. We walk through several small villages and then choose a slightly longer but more scenic route in order to miss the traffic and congestion of the highway into Burgos. A large, circular, concrete memorial to the Camino with its shell and modern depiction of a pilgrim greets us as we start into the outer reaches of the city. There are signs for the Camino everywhere we look: yellow arrows painted on trees, blue signs with yellow arrows on metal poles, brass shells imbedded in the sidewalks. There will be no getting lost in the maze of this city for us. It starts to rain, then pour. Eventually, the towering spires and pinnacles of the cathedral come into view. Although they are wrapped in mist, they are magnificent. Along with the waymarks, they are our guide into the central part of the city. Burgos, the capital of Castille, is a large, sprawling town. It takes us a long time to reach the old section at the cathedral. We have ducked into a bar for coffee to get out of the downpour and to fortify ourselves before we carry on. "No slippage!" I yell to Marcia laughingly, as we run in and out from under awnings by the storefronts and shops.

Fortunately, we come upon a municipal refugio that is located right on the Camino and just down the street from the cathedral complex. Ex-pilgrims are busily checking passports and pilgrim credentials and assigning bunk beds. Thankfully, two are going to us. This is a big operation here and a hub for those coming as well as leaving the Camino. We unpack and head out again to see the old city. The rain has almost stopped, so we walk carefully up the narrow street and descend down several flights of stairs to the Plaza de Santa Maria. We are intent on visiting the cathedral.

The French Gothic style, thirteenth-century Catedral de Santa Maria de Burgos (Cathedral of Saint Mary of Burgos) is gorgeous indeed. It houses a splendid mix of religious and medieval art and sculpture. Among the many treasures are the golden staircase, the graves of El Cid and his wife, Doña Jimena, and a large painting of Saint James, the Moor Slayer, his sword raised high as he rides his steed into battle. It would take two days to see it all properly, but we only have the end of the afternoon. We spend three hours here. In the early evening, we walk down the street to a charming restaurant we spotted earlier as we closed in on the refugio.

By dawn's light, we are already walking the two miles to the bus stop to catch a bus to the train station on the outskirts of town. We are heading north on the speed train to Paris. It is bittersweet to leave the Camino. I am consoling myself that I will hopefully be back next year to walk west again toward Santiago de Compostela. I am also horrified that I may have unwittingly slipped into the ranks of those "Camino junkies" who walk the path year after year. Never mind. *Call it all mui bueno*, I think to myself, as I gaze out the window of the train at the beauty that is Spain.

We have reserved a room for two nights at the Marriott on the west central side of Paris. I have to admit it is a relief to sink into the soft pillows and comforter at the hotel this evening. I also have to remind myself that I don't have to fill my pockets with toilet paper any more. Old habits die hard.

This morning, we are both excited to walk the streets of Paris again. We have taken the Metro to La Gare Montparnasse and are now heading by train to the Palace of Versailles. Marcia is indulging my wish to see it, although the fever quickly catches her too. We have to wait for almost two hours in a long line, in sweltering heat, to get in. It is worth it.

Louis the XIV, the Sun King, moved the French royal court from Paris in 1682 to the *Château de Versailles*, twelve miles west of the city. Thereafter, the Bourbon monarchs and their courtiers, the nobility lucky enough to establish themselves in the salons at the palace, remained there as the *Ancien Régime* until the French Revolution. As we move into *La Grande Galerie* (the famous Hall of Mirrors) with its splendor of sparkling crystal chandeliers, I wonder where Madame de Maintenon's chambers might have been? And as the royal musicians begin to play, I twirl around and around and around in the arms of the Sun King. But

Walking West on the Camino—Encore Une Fois   159

as the clock strikes down towards midnight, I drop his hand and run quickly away knowing full well that we will dance again someday in the heavens amid the twinkling stars. I am snapped back oh too soon into the flow of the crowd of sightseers moving me along out of the grand ballroom and the Hall of Mirrors to the interior rooms of the castle—and into the now.

Marcia and I tour the *Orangerie* next, which sits just under the windows of the castle in the back courtyard—this lovely garden with its fragrant pots of orange and lemon trees, pomegranates, and oleanders. Then, we walk down the long staircase to the Grand Canal and to the magnificent manicured groves and gardens of Versailles. I wonder—did I just catch a glimpse of the royal carriage? Or, was that the King on his promenade *à pied* strolling by the fountain of Apollo with his anxious courtiers trailing along behind him? And then, just as suddenly, they are gone.

We leave Versailles after walking its grounds for hours. We are exhausted, and we walk into the village itself to find a place to have an early dinner. *Bonsoir, Monsieur! Un grand pizza, salades vertes, et deux verres de vin rouge, s'il vous plait.* A pizza supper and salads are just the ticket for us this night. Of course, the main dining experience for the French happens much later in the evening, but by then, we will be long tucked into our beds back at our hotel.

This morning, we set off for the Paris Metro, which soon deposits us at a station near the *Musée du Moyen Âge* (the Cluny Museum). We exit the terminal and carry on until we reach Rue Saint Jacques and then Le Boulevard Saint Michel. *"Où est le Musée de Cluny?"* I had asked a nice French woman on the street. *Et voilà*, she points us in the direction with a smile. This museum is a magnificent repository of medieval sculpture and art, the most well known being the "Lady and the Unicorn" tapestries. We spend several hours here. By the afternoon, we have visited

Notre-Dame again and also the Église de Saint Severin. We dine outside under the red awnings of a café near the River Seine before catching the Metro back to the Marriott.

We have become quite proficient at maneuvering the Paris Metro. It wasn't always this way. Early on, on one of our adventures in Paris, I had attempted to force the doors of the subway back open with one of my hiking poles as Marcia had disappeared onto the subway car, and I was left standing on the platform, the door closing in my face. Just in the nick of time, I pulled out my pole, and the Metro pulled out *without me*. Angst ruled the day. Marcia and I were heading for the Paris Charles De Gaul Airport on the outskirts of town. I was able to catch the next train and got out at the first terminal (of several). Dejected, I was standing there wondering just how Marcia and I would reunite when I heard my name. Was it God calling me? No, not exactly. I turned around to see dear Marcia hurrying to me, excited and waving her arms.

By dawn, we are back again at the Charles De Gaul Airport heading for the United States. Thankfully, we have had no mishaps on the Metro this morning. I am going to say it yet again—*Oh la la!*

V.
Spring 2015
Burgos to León

105 MILES—8 DAYS

Burgos, Arroyo San Bol, Ermita San Nicholas, Villamentero de
Campos, Carrion de los Condes, Moratinos, Sahagún, Reliegos, León

*Keep me as the apple of the eye, hide me under the shadow of
thy wings.—Psalms 17:8*

It is hard to believe that a year has passed. Marcia and I have flown into Madrid and have taken the train to Burgos, where we left the Camino last year. We are both happy and excited to return. Even the familiarity of the train station comforts us. We catch the same commuter bus into the city and walk the two miles to the municipal refugio where we stayed last year. Fluffy white clouds are shielding the sun a bit in the heat of the afternoon.

After we check in and sort out our things, we walk up to the Burgos Cathedral for another view of its magnificent art and then explore some of the old district by the cathedral complex that we have not seen before. Burgos is a beautiful city. The trees are pollarded French style along a promenade of carousels and sculptured bushes and flower gardens. A mime is out hawking donations. She is dressed in a long red velvet gown, her face painted white. We stop for a while and order up that delectable Spanish treat of *churros con chocolate*. Yes, those greasy twisted donut sticks you dip into a cup of warm, thick chocolate. Or, should I say, *we* dip since by now we are seated outside in front of a café indulging ourselves. Have them once and no more, but *have them once!*

Later, we walk over to the same quaint restaurant where we ate last year and order from their peregrino menu: wonderful salmon, salads, crusty bread and olive oil, flan, and vino tinto. It is good to be back again. Pilgrims are appreciated along the Way here, and Spanish hospitality abounds. My heart sings a song of joy to walk the Camino once more.

As we leave Burgos this cool, crisp early morning, we cross down the street by ancient stone walls and then walk along through a commercial district out of the town. We have passed through several villages by now, walking the tranquil rhythms. The terrain is changing. We are starting into the meseta—a vast plateau of sky and fertile fields which some describe as a boring and laborious section of the Camino. For me, this area is quite the opposite. I find peace in the long expanse of nothingness. It is incredibly beautiful. But increasingly, the sun is blazing overhead in the bright blue sky. We can find no shade anywhere. We are walking down a narrow dirt tract through green fields and wild flowers as far as the eye can see. *Mariposas* (butterflies) are everywhere.

We stop in the village of Hornillos del Camino just long enough to sit down for a while by a fellow pilgrim named Angelique. She speaks some English and has a cell phone, and within minutes, she has called ahead and reserved two spaces for us at the refugio at San Bol. She is staying there too, she tells us. Shangra-la! We had just begun to wonder rather anxiously about where we might spend the night. The Camino is packed with hikers. By the time we reach San Bol, we have come almost sixteen miles today.

Beautiful Arroyo San Bol—only an angel could have arranged such a place as this for us. Interestingly enough, Angelique isn't staying here, and we never see her again.

This small stone albergue sits just off the Camino, down a dirt road to the left, by a stream and a grove of tall poplars. A large white scallop shell with a red crusader's cross has been painted on the side of the building, and a round stone roof sits on top of it all. It is an oasis of sorts on the meseta, I suspect, as it has been for centuries. In medieval times, the Antonin monks set up a pilgrim hospital here at the hamlet then known as San Baudilio. There was also a leper colony nearby. All that remains today is the refugio. A gracious young Spanish woman checks our pilgrim credentials and shows us to our bunk beds. There is room for twelve souls here and no more. We shower and unpack and then join the ranks of other pilgrims who are sitting on the porch and in the yard enjoying the last of the warmth of the late afternoon sun. Marcia and I sit under the trees and dip our sore and achy feet into the cool spring water. It is said to have healing properties.

By dinnertime, we find ourselves seated at a round wooden table in the small dining room under a beautiful, circular black-iron chandelier. The walls of this room have been delicately crafted in stone, and the high, dome-shaped ceiling is painted a smoky blue. A German couple has joined us among the others, and Marcia speaks some of her long-lost German with them for a moment. She lived in Berlin many years ago, just before the wall came down. And, our host places the most scrumptious huge pan of paella in the middle of the table, right under our noses. Exuberance rings out in various languages. "*Salud!*" We all exclaim as we lift our glasses of vino tinto high. Indeed, God has

Wheat fields on the Meseta as far as the eye can see

blessed us our first day back on the road to Santiago de Compostela.

A thin glimmer of light stretches across the horizon as the sun is rising amidst low hanging purple-gray clouds. The moon is higher up and still visible as a small white hazy orb in the blue sky. As we leave San Bol, we are again walking down the narrow, dirt, ribbon-like road that is the Camino. It stretches across the green valley and plateau for miles and miles. What a lovely morning it is for a walk. About three miles along, we reach Hontanas. The beautiful bell tower of its church looms high, dominating this picturesque little village nestled in the valley. As we carry on through the village, we meet up with two American women. A mother and her young adult daughter are walking a portion of the Camino together. We strike up a conversation as we walk. The woman is from Washington state; both she and her husband are attorneys there. She, coincidentally, has been practicing child welfare law for years just as I have. She confirms what I already know and can reflect back to her: it is a breath of fresh air and a relief to take a break from it all and to sojourn on the Camino. They then continue on as Marcia and I have stopped on the side of the road to rest our feet and backs and drink water.

Our walking guide recommends that we stay on the tree-lined road all the way to Castrojeriz. Shade is good, believe me, in the heat of this day. Several more miles down the road, we reach the remains of the Gothic Hospital San Antón and its refugio. A young priest is just riding up on his bicycle and, smiling, he invites us to step around the old walls of the hospital and see the newly refurbished refugio for pilgrims. It is spartan, but it offers a sweet and welcoming refuge for those who stop here. We sit down among the hospital ruins and tall trees for our own respite, and I think about those who may have passed this way and found rest and even healing. French monks here were said to have cured some of those unfortunate souls sick with Ergotism, or St. Anthony's Fire—that horrid condition which we had heard about as we passed along the Le Puy Route in St. Antoine. They are said to have used a special t-shaped Tau cross when praying for the sick; we see the Tau cross at the top of the bell tower of the old church as we walk on.

We pass under an archway and, after two or three more miles down the dirt road, we reach Castrojeriz. The ruins of a majestic old castle stand high on a hill overlooking the village. Most likely, the castle's fort offered protection in the Middle Ages and as far back as Celtic times. This village has been a major pilgrim halt through the centuries and still is. Unfortunately, the Gothic church of Nuestra Señora del Manzano, which is said to have an image of Our Lady of the Apple Tree as well as one of St. James, is locked. So are the other churches. Here it is again—*the apple*. After we have walked through the village, our winding route crosses a bald plateau uphill. A large cairne stands at the summit as another monument to the many pilgrims who have passed this way. We ourselves stand in awe, looking across the valley and surveying the next part of our journey. It will take us down a narrow path through an expanse of bright green fields. Wild red poppies and white posies line the road.

About a mile or two farther, we reach the thirteenth-century Ermita San Nicholas, a former pilgrim hospital. This pristine old stone building has since been converted into a refugio by the *Confraternita dei San Jacopo*, the Italian Association of St. James. We have walked almost sixteen miles today and to say we are fortunate to get two beds here would be an understatement. The next village is almost seven miles away. We are "the apples of God's eye" yet again.

This refugio, with its high stone ceiling and archway inside, has bunk beds, with red sheets and pillowcases, lining the walls on the first floor. They sit just by a long table where we will be served dinner tonight and café con leche and bread tomorrow morning. A small chapel adjoins the master room with gold and red icons of Jesus, Mary, and Saint Nicholas set up on the altar. Just above them, the sun shines diffused soft light into the refugio from a high narrow window. It is serene and beautiful. And this is where we will sleep tonight—it is hard to fathom. Marcia and I sit outside in the afternoon sun by lilac bushes for a long while resting our weary feet. At dinner, we are served plates of pasta bolognese along with salads, bread, and red wine. A pilgrim mass is held afterwards, and one of the association brothers (who has donned a dark red cape with two scallop shells and a red crusader's cross emblazoned on the front) washes the feet of every peregrino. They take their call to humble service very seriously here, in a long tradition of healing those who walk the Way. These prayer-soaked old hospital walls stand silent, but we all know, just the same.

As the sun rises this morning, we have already crossed the bridge over the River Piserga and have walked through the next small village of Itero de la Vega. Marcia is noticing a bright red circle the size of a silver dollar forming on her leg just above her ankle. "Now just what is this?" she asks, with some amount of alarm—rightly so. In the next village of Frómista we are able to find a medical office that is open, and in due time, we are heading to a pharmacy nearby to fill a prescription for a strong antibiotic cream, just in case this is a tick bite. We also pass by the church, but it is closed. It seems the beauty of the Camino itself is our holy chapel this day. We merely have to look to the rolling clouds and blue sky and to the green fields and poppies as we wind our way along. By late afternoon, we have found sweet refuge for the night in the small village of Villarmentero de Campos. Sleep comes easily for us both. We have walked almost ten miles today—quite enough. Thankfully, the red of Marcia's bug bite is fading too.

Today's route takes us by the road on a long straight footpath alongside cornfields. We eventually reach Carrión de los Condes after about ten miles. In earlier days, this town was another major halt on the Camino. Still a hub in this region of Palencia in Castille y Leon, it is a beautiful, busy place. I am intent on finding a shop where I can purchase some hiking sandals. My toes have been complaining loudly for days on end. I just haven't told *you* too much about it until now so as not to appear so whiny. A large mosaic image of St. James on the side of a building greets us as we walk into the town. We visit the Convento de Santa Clara and its refugio to the left just as we start through the village and then decide to walk on. And yes, I am now the proud owner of a lovely pair of blue and grey hiking sandals, which I found in a small shoe store. My toes are singing a tune of relief. We have also located two more refugios, but both of them are full. Our path is taking us around to leave the village, and we still have no place to stay. The next village of Calzadilla de la Cueza, almost eleven miles away, is not an option. Oh no!

Marcia and I are both literally praying for and expecting a miracle. It comes swiftly. A Spanish woman is just leaving an alberque (booked solid too), and after our inquiry as to where we might stay, she points us up the street past a barricade and over to the large convent of the Filipenses, the Casa de Espiritualidad. It was not visible from the road, nor was it listed in our guidebook. It is also off the Camino a block or two. But, why should I be amazed at our good fortune? Well, I just am nonetheless—amazed and awed!

This convent keeps rooms for pilgrims as part of their service to the community and to the Camino. We are delighted. As we check in, word spreads that two Americans are there, and it is then that Sister Edith rushes up, smiling. She introduces herself in perfect English. She is an American citizen who was sent to the Filipenses convent in Cuba for many years and then was re-assigned here. She is overjoyed to converse with Americans, and we are overjoyed she speaks English. It is a happy combination all around.

Sister Edith shows us to a small private room up three floors. We have two simple wooden beds complete with crisp white sheets and blankets and a separate small bathroom. It reminds me of what a monastic cell might look like. But to us, it is the Taj Mahal. After our showers, we go via an elevator to the basement laundry room, where we wash our dusty, dirty clothes in large machines. A door leads out back to a grassy courtyard and clotheslines. A peregrino mule is parked in the shade there, apparently on pilgrimage too. We dig out more apples and have soon easily made another furry friend.

Later, we are served a lovely dinner of lightly fried fish, french-fries, salads, bread, and red wine by one of the nuns on kitchen duty tonight. We then walk next door to the beautiful old stone church for a pilgrim mass. Back again in our cell, we have no TV, no telephone, no cell phone, no internet. I could retire here and live out my days in peace. But, of course, I know it is not to be. I also know, rather wistfully, that I will be only too soon back home again, surfing the net and flipping TV channels to PBS.

By morning, dear Sister Edith is delivering up big hugs as she sees us off. It is another beautiful sunny day. We cross the bridge at the Río Carrión and walk straight ahead for miles and miles through several small villages until we get to Terradillos de los Templarios, a village long ago established by the Knights Templar. The church here is closed, as have been other churches we have passed this day. The two large refugios are full and overflowing. We are forced to carry on to Moratinos, which is another two miles. By then, we will have walked almost eighteen miles today. But I notice this—I am up to the task and invigorated by our unfolding adventure. It is interesting to see how my mind and body rally when continuing on becomes the only option. Adrenalin (and insanity) have also kicked in. Our book lists no refugios in Moratinos and only one in the next village of San Nicholas (another mile or two away). The sun has dropped down to kiss the earth. A deep pink blush forming on the horizon signals us to pick up our pace. Shall I say, we are both becoming a bit delirious. We begin to laugh and sing and skip down the "yellow brick road" to tunes from The Wizard of Oz like the two little girls we once were. On and on we go until we finally reach the tiny village of Moratinos and the best surprise of all—the Hospital San Bruno.

Yes, we are bunking down this night with Bruno (not literally) at his alberque Italian-style. The place is filling up fast, but we manage to get two spaces in a large dormitory-style room full of bunk beds. I have the bottom bunk and Marcia the top. Bruno sells bug spray (never a good sign), but we decline. Word has gotten around again that Americans are staying here. Soon enough, a kindly British gentleman steps up to introduce himself and asks if he can interview us about our reasons for walking the Camino. I think to myself, *Oh good, maybe he can tell me why I am here!* We say the usual things: we love to hike; we like to walk together; we love to sit in the beautiful churches; Marcia can say I *made* her go (at least initially) until she caught the bug (not bed bugs) too. I didn't think to ask him at the time to please ask dear God why we are here and get back with me.

Patrick and his American wife, Rebekah Scott, have retired from the newspaper business and are free-lance journalists. They have invited us over. We walk the short distance to their lovely home, called "Peaceable Kingdom," and share good conversation as well as good Spanish red wine. Rebekah has just finished a novel, rooted in the history and folklore of the region, called *The Moorish Whore*. It is the delightful tale of King Alfonso VI and his legendary mistress Zeida, a princess plucked from the Moors, in Seville. I can't wait to read it! They have rescued several stray dogs; their home is a menagerie of sorts. We meet and greet the dogs too, their tails wagging furiously. It is not lost on either Marcia or me that we were not supposed to stay at those jam-packed refugios behind us—that we had signed up for this much more interesting and sweet occasion with new friends, however brief. Life is such a mystery, so much of which I do not understand and most likely never will. We return to our refugio early enough for the pilgrim meal served up especially by Bruno (his pasta is superb) and then drag ourselves to bed.

Our goal is to reach the large town of Sahagún, which is only six miles away. We want to rest today, hopefully at the Convent of the Madres Benedictinas. First, we have to get there. As we leave the province of Polencia and enter that of Leon, we walk through the village of San Nicholas and come to the Ermita Virgen del Puente, a former pilgrim hospice now closed. Taking a sharp left, we cross an old stone bridge and walk along a flat dirt path until we get to Sahagún. At the convent there, we ring the bell and finally we are greeted by a woman who clearly wasn't expecting pilgrims so early in the day. Nevertheless, we are assigned a private room with two little beds. Per the sign on the door, the convent books rooms for pilgrims at their one-star hotel. This is great for us. Soon enough, the rooms for pilgrims are filling up. After we regroup, we sun ourselves on the balcony of the inner courtyard. Wet wash (ours included) is hanging everywhere on clotheslines. Below in the courtyard, beautiful tall white hydrangea bushes form the centerpiece amid white tables and chairs. We have picked a peaceful spot and a haven from the heat of the day.

By late afternoon, we have explored the old section of town including the ruins of a Benedictine Monastery founded by the monks of Cluny. We then stop for an early supper and sit outside in the town square. We order a large salade niçoise. A young (it turns out American) woman, who is walking around looking somewhat lost, gratefully accepts our invitation to join us and to share our salad. It is funny how the Camino invites all kinds of brief and yet open and intense encounters among the pilgrims, each of us sharing our stories and then, just as easily, moving on. It reminds me of meeting someone on an airplane and conversing about what matters deeply much too quickly (what my niece calls giving TMI—too much information). Then, we disembark and never think a thing about it again. Although I must say, these days I myself prefer to say little on airplanes. I seem to want my privacy and peace most of all.

Marcia and I are fortunate in that we have a great time walking together on the Camino. We share a lot of camaraderie, although sometimes it is unfortunately at the exclusion of others. I also recognize another downside—that neither of us gets to walk alone. I mean *really alone* for miles and miles, hour upon hour. It is then, I believe, one might draw closest to God—in the sublime silence. Marcia and I could separate, of course, and meet up later, but neither of us really wants to. We both prefer to savor our time together—it is so fleeting. Then I think that, maybe, we are destined to walk the Camino together and this is just okay. Someday, I do hope to walk other portions of the Camino in France alone, in holy solitude, as a walking meditation—an empty vessel. And then, I muse about whom I might encounter, even St. James himself, as he gently takes my hand to walk west. After all, the Great Apostle entreats us to get wisdom and to have undivided faith, and that there is a divine order even in the chaos, and divine timing.

We walk across and down the street to the church for a pilgrim blessing and vespers. The nuns sing songs of joy, unlike the melancholy refrains we have heard in other churches. I too prefer to focus on hope and to trust that God will make all things right. And with that, we return for the night and prepare for tomorrow's new day.

As we head out this morning, we walk down to the Río Cea and cross an old bridge to leave Sahagún. A huge stone cross and a large bronze pilgrim's staff and gourd mark the passage out of town. We are walking along a flat, tree-lined gravel track just off the road. Our guidebook informs us so helpfully that this is the area where a seventeenth-century pilgrim came upon the body of another who had been eaten by wolves. Marcia had read on the internet that there were supposedly no bears on the Camino, so she was much relieved. But neither of us read the fine print about *wolves*—until now. I wonder if they like cat food and if they would oblige us the time to get it out of our packs, or if we might have to shimmy up a tree or something? Just some pleasant thoughts of mine as I am surveying the landscape. No need for alarm—yet.

Almost nine miles along, we have walked through two small villages (with no wolf sightings) and then, having come to the little village of El Burgo Ranero, we stop for our customary picnic lunch. We have found shade on the porch at their lovely old church. The church itself is locked. Storks have claimed the bell tower, and they are perched in their nests getting a bird's eye view of us as we eat. It is a sweet spot. I wonder if a lot of these churches in Spain are closed during the intense heat of the day only to reopen after five o'clock, after their siesta. By that hour, we are winding down just as the locals are winding up for activity late into the evening.

As we carry on, we are walking again on another shaded dirt track. Cows are grazing under the poplar trees just across the road, in grassy fields. Eventually, we reach the village of Reliegos, where we book for the night at the Albergue and Restaurante La Parada. Painted a dark sunlit gold, the albergue fairly glows in the late afternoon sun. For dinner, we are served plates of fried fish and salade niçoise, after which we stroll around this picturesque town—me with leftover fish in napkins stuffed in my pocket. Maybe this is TMI again, but yes, I end up feeding more ravenous cats. This time it is two little semi-wild kittens crouched on someone's porch. Do unto man (and beast) as you would have it done unto you.

Our path this morning zigzags across fields, then goes on by the side of the road and across a long footbridge over the highway, until almost sixteen miles later, we reach beautiful bustling León, our final destination for this year's pilgrimage. It takes us eons to get to the old section of the city. We cross the bridge at the rushing Río Torío and walk up through the city central, always following the yellow shells. We are headed for the Convento Santa Maria de la Carbajales, a Benedictine convent, on the Plaza de Santa Maria—like homing pigeons. Or should I say, storks? We have read that this convent houses and cares for large numbers of pilgrims coming through León. This afternoon is no exception. There are lines already forming to sign up for the refugio and for the pilgrim meal for tonight. The nuns and lay volunteers alike are busy checking us all in. We manage to reserve two bunks, dinner, and our customary small breakfast.

My feet are sore. Marcia's are too, but she refuses the kindly offer of a cold foot bath. Apparently, it is the panacea for all that ails pilgrim feet. I soon find this to be true, but only as long as my sore toes and achy feet stay plunged in the icy water, half-frozen. Marcia insists that she would rather have sore feet than get some fungus lurking in those plastic tubs. Nevertheless, our ever so helpful hosts (two older lay volunteers) just laugh it up and dance a gig by our bunk beds, one with an empty washtub balanced on top of his head. It is a new-fangled pilgrim hat or something. After all, laughter is the best medicine.

Maybe the path to enlightenment is laughter. If so, I should be a saint by now. But then, you would have to laugh at everything—the good, the bad, and the ugly. And, if all is an illusion here anyway, and our real home is in the ethereal realms, well go ahead and laugh it up! I suspect, however, that it is the other way around—that seeking God first and turning within in whatever way, through prayer and meditation, brings the light and then the laughter. I also suspect that enlightenment can come even without our grasping or seeking after it at all—through God's grace. Maybe it comes through suffering too. King David beseeched God for illumination many times in the Psalms: "Quicken me, O Lord," he wrote. Saint Teresa wrote in *The Interior Castle* that our efforts will carry us only so far, and then God must step in. Did I manage to drop my guidebook for Planet Earth somewhere between Orion's Belt and Jupiter? I want it back right now!

Early this morning, we have had our *café con leche y tostado* (coffee and toast) and are headed back across the city to the train station. Leaving the Camino is a sweet and surreal sorrow, but we want to fit in some more excursions at the end of this year's trip to Spain. We are hoping to book two seats for Avila, which is just northwest of Madrid on the train line south from Leon. Our Carmelite friends back home gently nudged us this direction. It didn't take much. With my ticket now in hand, I sink into my seat on the train, grateful just to sit and rest my feet for a few hours and do nothing.

Once in Avila, we have managed to get walking directions to the old section of town. We walk a couple of miles on the sidewalk by a long park and then through the busy modern commercial district to the ancient walled city. Avila is the birthplace of Saint Teresa, the great Christian mystic and first female doctor of the Catholic Church, whom I have mentioned before. St. Teresa wrote of her ecstasies in union with God. She was a feminine voice hampered by the restrictions of her age, but unrestricted in her spiritual life. Avila is also home to her male counterpart, Saint John of the Cross, who so famously wrote of the *dark night of the soul* in the Christian mystical traditions. The old part of the city fairly seeps with the history of their devotion and spiritual teachings.

As we step through the turreted medieval wall at the Alcazar Gate into Saint Teresa's past, we walk down those same narrow cobblestone streets she must have tread. Unfortunately, the dark, silver, granite Gothic Cathedral of Avila is covered in scaffolding at the front for structural repairs. It is also locked. We walk on. It is early afternoon, and we want to eat and also find a place to stay. The old city is bustling with activity. We eventually find a two-star hotel located just off the Plaza Mayor. And, we eat a late lunch outside at one of the plaza restaurants. Avila is brimming with added excitement. This year commemorates the five-hundredth birthday of St. Teresa. Her picture is everywhere announcing the celebratory event.

By now, we are anxious to walk the streets to the far end of the walled town to visit the Carmelitas Descalzos "La Santa," the Convent of Saint Teresa of Jesus and its church. We are in luck, for it is open. The church houses gorgeous, colorful stained glass art depicting St. Teresa's life. The one I find most alluring is that of the Saint seated at her wooden desk, writing. A dove (symbolizing the Holy Spirit) hovers just above her, its rays of bright white light piercing her veil. I sit in this most peaceful and holy place for a long while, unruffled by time or space, until I realize we have more to see in this lovely city, and the evening is encroaching on our limited time here.

We are also fortunate to visit the Museo de Santa Teresa located just down from the church in the crypt of the Monastery of Friars. This is the very site where St. Teresa was born and where she lived her early life. I find it fascinating—especially her monastic cell reproduced from the original at Saint Joseph's Convent (also in Avila). This "saintly wanderer" set about bringing needed reform to the Carmelite Order of nuns and friars and also founded various monasteries in Spain. A replica of her woven sandals is shown, from which the reformed order of

Discalced Carmelites gets its name—*discalced* meaning to go barefoot or wear sandals only.

After we emerge from the museum crypt, we climb a grassy hill and walk up a stone staircase to the edge of the city wall and then cross through a door into the exterior grounds, but not before snapping pictures of this stately old doorway as it meets the bright blue sky. I ask Marcia with a certain amount of awe, "I wonder if St. Teresa walked this way and looked out this door as we do now." (Our Carmelite friends back home must think so too, because our photos of this beautiful portal to the heavens almost brought them to their knees—they were so entranced.) We are looking out over a wide expanse of the river valley. And next, we walk down the hill to the shady lane below and meander by the fortifications and ramparts until we reach the Alcazar Gate once more, to head back to the hotel.

We are oh so glad to have a hotel room this night and real sheets and towels. It is time to do nothing again—blessed nothing. Now this reminds me of what Mother told us when we were little. "Arise and shine," she would say, as she came into our bedroom to raise the shades. "June around!" This is Southern for "You better get your chores done and get about your day." I have been *juning around* ever since, sometimes to my detriment, it seems. Busy, busy, busy. I suspect St. Teresa would simply tell me to sit down and shut up and focus on my breath, let my monkey-mind thoughts just pass through, and enter the holy silence (not exactly in those words). Perhaps the Camino orders up this very thing, and it is one reason I love to walk it so much.

After breakfast at the hotel, we retrace our steps, leaving the charming walled city of old Avila, and walk the few miles back to the train station. We barely scratched the surface of what we might see here and missed out on seeing the cathedral and various other magnificent churches and monasteries made famous by St. Teresa and St. John of the Cross. I have to drag myself away. Unfortunately, we have run out of time, and we must press on to Segovia. Another UNESCO World Heritage Site, the old walled city of Segovia, just north of Madrid, dates back to Celtic and then Roman times. We don't want to miss it.

Once in Segovia, we walk a mile or two to get into the central part of the city and the old section. We have located a tourist information center and find ourselves soon enough standing in line waiting for an English speaking young woman behind the desk to help us. The good news is that it is Friday afternoon, and the city is preparing to host an annual international puppet festival for the weekend. Colorful vendors and puppeteers are out in mass on the narrow streets. The festivities are just getting underway. The bad news is that Segovia is booked solid with tourists and festival goers. And just as we turn away to leave the tourist office, the girl recommends offhand that we should check out a hostel located just down the street. "Go left under the Roman aqueduct and down a long flight of stone stairs, and you will see it on the left," she tells us with a hopeful smile and some excitement. We go quickly, hoping upon hope we will find beds there. Sound familiar? We are now on the Camino called *life*.

Those beautiful, brilliant, never bashful, booking angels take over from here. No sooner do we get to the hostel than we find that someone has just called in to cancel. We get the last two beds. I couldn't make this up if I tried. A bilingual young man at his desk is just finishing the phone call. Well, we could complain like spoiled little children that we are in yet another spartan refugio where we are assigned *bunk beds,* or we could jump for joy. We choose the latter. My feet are thanking me profusely as we are fawning over our host. This kind fellow is obviously taking pleasure in helping us. I am reminded of an old admonition about kindness. Years ago, a new friend of mine lay dying in the hospital from a massive overdose of chemotherapy. Propped up on his pillow, he had no bitterness or regret in his voice, only a gentle sorrow, as he whispered, "Be kind." It was sage advice from a dying man. Our young host practices it well.

We are out to explore Segovia now, having secured beds for the night and having dumped our backpacks and poles—beautiful Segovia. We retrace our steps up the long stone staircase and walk by a statue of Romulus and Remus and the she-wolf and then walk under the Roman aqueduct to return to what we now know is the Plaza del Azoguejo—and a huge street fair. A brightly painted carousel, lit up and twirling with whimsical animals, stands center-stage just by the aqueduct. The puppeteers are already out in the streets and delighting the crowds. Marcia and I stroll the cobblestone passageways, going in and out of storefronts and pottery shops, finally settling on some hand-painted olive dishes and wine-bottle stoppers to take home to friends. After all, it is a lovely, warm, sunny day to be a tourist.

We are winding our way along to reach, eventually, the sixteenth-century Gothic Cathedral of Segovia, located right on the Plaza Mayor, where Isabella I was proclaimed Queen of Castile. The cathedral's tall, glittering spires encircle a bell tower. They fairly dance in the light against the azure-blue sky. We sit inside for a long while amidst some of the most beautiful stained glass windows that I have ever seen—many are dedicated to the Virgin Mary. We then have lunch outside at a small restaurant on the Plaza Mayor.

Intent on visiting the Alcázar of Segovia next, we walk on. Built in the Middle Ages by Moorish kings, the castle sits high on a huge rock formation overlooking the valley, at the confluence of two rivers. It was the fortress of the Kings of Castile. We read that it is still the part-time residence of the current Spanish King. It is also rumored to have served as the inspiration for Disney's Cinderella fairy-tale castle. We can see why as we approach it. The alcázar, with its turrets and glistening, slate-gray, pointed towers, stands majestically as a grand sentinel overlooking the city. We sit on a rocky outcropping at a distance for a long time taking photos and just admiring its splendor.

Once inside, we roam its stately chambers and halls, admiring its art as well as its collection of knights' armor and weaponry—eerie echoes of days past. Standing out on one of its many balconies, we can see for miles and miles, even in the late afternoon haze. We walk its magnificent and shady gardens and then head home. Yes, home to our refugio.

As the sun is setting and the old city is just lighting up, we walk to the restaurant, El Segoviano, to have our last supper in Spain. It sits just by the Roman aqueduct. We dine on a tasty, thick, white bean casserole popular in the region and called in Spanish *judiones de la granja*, a salad, course bread with olive oil, and vino tinto. For dessert, we have the traditional *tarta de Santiago*, or almond cake, a favorite on the Camino as you enter the Galician region. Back in my little bed, I drift into happy sleep. Our Spanish female roommates, who have come to Segovia for the puppet festival, are coming and going. I am oblivious to it all.

This morning, Marcia and I check out early. We have much more to see before we take the train back to Madrid. Armed with a map of the city, we pass through the ramparts and make our way down a narrow, shady road toward outlying churches and monasteries we had seen yesterday as we stood on the hill at the alcázar surveying the landscape below.

One that we both find most interesting is the Iglesia de la Vera Cruz (the Church of the True Cross). This twelve-sided church was founded in the thirteenth century by the Knights of the Holy Sepulchre, though legend has it that it was an early Knights Templar church. The twelve sides represent the twelve apostles. It is now occupied by the Order of the Knights of Malta. Inside, we are met by rows of flags hung high portraying the crusaders cross as well as the royal *fleur de lis*. A beautiful old *retablo* of paintings depicting the life of Christ stands in the back. We climb the long staircase to the second floor to find a large stone altar placed in the middle of a circular room with a domed ceiling. A painting of the Virgin Mary, her soulful sad eyes cast down, hangs on one wall. She wears a red cape lined in green. It is an unusual depiction of Mary which I find to be hauntingly captivating.

We also visit the church associated with a Carmelite Convent named after San Juan de la Cruz. A gold statue of the Blessed Mary in front of an indigo mosaic background is particularly striking. St. Teresa and St. John of the Cross are also depicted through statues and in paintings along the walls. Magnificent tall cedars line the stone walkway and staircase down to the street.

We walk on until we reach the train station again, where we purchase tickets for Madrid, the last leg on this year's journey. We have booked two nights at the Airport Hilton. Madrid is an easy hour or less on the train from Segovia. Once there, we manage to get information at the Chamartin station on how to get first to the Puerta del Sol Square and then to the old Plaza Mayor. Before long, we are walking the perimeter of the Plaza Mayor and deciding on a tapas bar just off the Plaza, the Naviego, for a late lunch. Coincidentally, this is the same tapas bar I had visited many years ago when I was last in Madrid. We order up crispy calamari, assorted olives, garlic pimientos de Patron, and thick slices of Spanish bread for dipping in olive oil. Next, we walk the old cobbled street into the area of restaurants and tapas bars that Hemmingway frequented and made famous. Later, we check in at the Hilton. Its luxury is a far cry from the refugios we have slept in over the course of our travels on the Camino. I think I like the simplicity and quiet hospitality of the refugios as much as this fine hotel. They are just different experiences, that's all.

This is our day to see more of Madrid. It is a beautiful sunny morning. We have taken a bus into the city central, taking care to note where we will need to catch the bus again to return to the hotel this evening. We walk past the Bank of Spain, which must cover two large city blocks, heading for the Thyssen Museum, where we spend several hours. We then stroll past the fountain of Cybele and then the fountain of Neptune, dodging traffic, until we reach the Buen Retiro Park. Once there, we snap photos of the Monument to Alfonso XII which sits just across the lake. People are out in small blue rowboats enjoying the scenery and whiling away the day. Next, we walk to the famous Prado Museum, but by now it is early afternoon and we decide not to go in, and instead visit a beautiful church nearby.

For a late lunch, we stop in a café and then walk several long blocks through the city to the Temple of Debod, an ancient Egyptian temple which was dismantled and rebuilt in Madrid. Only several hours later do I notice that I am missing my waist belt and, oh yes, my debit and credit cards, not to mention some cash and a favorite silver ring. Panic sets in. We retrace our steps back to the café where we had lunch, the only place I could have left it, but to no avail. By now, I am beside myself. It gets worse. We, who had taken such care to remember our bus stop to catch the bus back to the Hilton, now find ourselves walking around and around the area of the Bank of Spain and the museums, unable to recognize it. This goes on for at least an hour until a nice woman at a tourist information booth points us to the right location for the bus stop.

Back again at the Hilton and with the help of the concierge, I am fortunately able to call and cancel my two bank cards so that no further mischief can occur. Fresh off the Camino, I do not feel charmed anymore. In fact, I sink into my covers by nightfall in abject tears from the stress of it all. I realize that there is war everywhere, people are dying and starving on this planet. My misadventures this afternoon pale in comparison. I cry anyway. I am looking for some way to "call it all good," but it has escaped me.

I wish I had my guidebook to Planet Earth. It has probably gone the way of my money belt. And, no amount of "divine inaction" will recover it. Then it occurs to me—what else is left to do but laugh? After all, what choice do I have? And perhaps the bigger miracle is that I had moved my passport and driver's license to my zipped jacket pocket earlier this morning. Go figure. So, tomorrow morning we are flying back to the States after a lovely trip to Spain and to the Camino. I have to tell myself again—*get a grip!* Let's just say, I am both sad and relieved to go home.

VI.
Spring 2016
León to Santiago de Compostela

185 MILES—13 DAYS

León, San Martin del Camino, Astorga, Rabanal del Camino,
Molinaseca, Villafranca del Bierzo, Ruitelan, Fonfria, Samos,
Ferreiros, Portomarin, Ventas de Naron, Melide, Arzua, Arca,
Santiago de Compostela

Thou will show me the path of life: in thy presence is fullness of joy.
—Psalms 16:11

This year, we are looking forward to completing the Camino and reaching Santiago de Compostela. I am excited and also a bit sad that our six-year excursion will end only too soon. It is more about the *process*, I realize, than about reaching the *destination* on any pilgrimage or journey. But, I do so much want Marcia to experience Santiago and its beautiful Cathedral as I did many years ago.

We have flown into Madrid and have made our way via the Metro over to Chamartin station to take the train to León, where we left off last year. I have booked ahead both the train tickets and our first night's stay. The Camino is becoming more and more popular with Americans since the release of the movie *The Way* as well as blogs and documentaries about the pilgrimage. Besides the Camino's general increase in pilgrims, the Camino Frances, the portion of the Camino which starts at the French border in the Pyrenees and crosses Spain, is a convergence of several Camino routes and is the most traveled.

About booking ahead: it is not that I would mind sleeping under the stars if we can't find beds, it is just that I am not interested in doing so *tonight*! Now, Marcia is rolling her eyes. Well okay, I am not interested in camping out *any night*, not with those wolves and snakes and chickens creeping up as soon as the sun goes down. Or, did I mention that one old man whom we met on the trail who kindly posed for a photo with Marcia and then promptly planted a big kiss on her mouth, much to her dismay? Payoff time, I guess. Or, how about that sweet looking older gentleman I happened to plop down next to on a bench, for a rest, who then patted my behind when I stood up to carry on. Oh, I forgot, I doubt very much that those old gentlemen are out after dark.

We have flown all night having met up again in the Atlanta Airport. Jetlag has set in, as I knew it would before I booked our hotel weeks ago. We will want a good night's sleep tonight, free from the snores and sneezes of our fellow peregrinos. We are staying at the three-star Hospedería Monástica Pax in old León, right on the Camino—the very same place I refused to stay in last year. Marcia had wanted us to stay there, but we had opted for the refugio next door at my insistence. I guess I was being my monkish self again. Yet, I felt bad about it, and so I wish to oblige Marcia this year and, really, myself too. The Pax is a sweet hotel attached to the Convento Santa Maria de la Carbajales and its refugio.

A walking map of León in hand, we have crossed the bridge over the Río Torío at the perimeter of the city and are heading for the Plaza Santa Maria del Camino and our hotel. I wonder about myself and the allure the Camino still holds for me. I am so excited that I can barely contain myself. I am also happy to see Marcia again. We are both giggling up the sidewalk, two grown women, sixty-five *today* as a matter of fact! Our trusty old hiking poles and backpacks are on high alert, having been called into service again. I imagine our angels have been called up for active duty too and are following along just behind us. I cannot be trusted to be very sane right now, or am I just sleep-deprived? We are already having such fun.

Once at the Pax, we settle in and reserve a pilgrim meal at the restaurant, which is associated with both the hotel and the refugio. Excitement is the order of the night at dinner. There are those at our table who are just starting out, as well as those who have been hiking for weeks on end. We are seated family-style among French pèlerins, all of us happy to press on tomorrow. It is great to be back.

~⚜~

Just after dawn, we have already had our pilgrim breakfast of café con leche y tostado and are walking through the old part of León. Our guidebook routes us by the French Gothic Cathedral of León (unfortunately not open yet) to eventually leave the city by a grand old hotel or parador, formally the Romanesque Church of San Marcos. Fellow pilgrims are congregating outside the hotel around their taxis with mounds of luggage. No backpacking for them, it seems. We walk on.

Almost five miles later, we reach Virgen del Camino (really a suburb of León since we never left sidewalks or storefronts) and its modern Church of San Froilan. Huge bronze statues of the twelve apostles, as well as of the Virgin Mary, stand outside high on the church's front facade. St. James is among them, pointing the way to Santiago de Compostela. *Just who is St. Froilan?* I wonder. Saint Froilan, the patron saint of the province of León, was the bishop of León in the year 900. He brought Benedictine monasticism to this part of northwestern Spain, which had been wrested away from the Moors.

We rest in the side chapel of the church and admire a beautiful painting of Our Lady of Guadalupe. I am quite familiar with her image, having lived in northern New Mexico for years, as well as having visited her shrine in Mexico City years ago. Our Lady of Guadalupe is the patron saint of the Americas. She is said to have appeared several times to an Aztec Indian named Juan Diego in 1531 in central Mexico. His cloak, imprinted with her image, bore witness to the apparitions. The painting, aglow with stars twinkling on Mary's dark blue cape, is undeniably beautiful and captivating.

Shortly past the church, we have a choice of routes, both way-marked. We choose the slightly shorter route that passes more often by the road—okay by us. We walk through several hamlets to eventually reach the small village of San Martin del Camino. We have come almost fourteen miles—quite enough for our first day back. We are fortunate to find beds and meals at an auberge for a total of eighteen euros operated and owned by a young bilingual woman from Brazil and her Spanish husband. Fellow pilgrims are out on the terrace and in the courtyard basking in the late afternoon sun. Bed space is filling up fast by now, as usual. Our hosts are already busy preparing dinner: a huge steaming seafood and chicken paella and fresh green salad. They tell us that they prepare this tasty dish every night as a matter of convenience and because it is the perfect dish for the many cycles of pilgrims who stay for a night and then walk on. We are again seated family-style at long tables, this time with a friendly group of hikers from Spain and South America. My bunk bed is calling my name soon after we eat—no surprise. I retire to peruse my walking guide once more.

This morning, we have set our sights on Astorga, almost twelve miles away. After about four-and-a-half miles, we come

Walking West on the Camino—Encore Une Fois

Our Lady of Guadalupe

to a long bridge over the River Orbigo which will take us into the village of Hospital de Orbigo just ahead. This old cobblestone bridge, the longest pilgrim bridge in Spain, has its own interesting history. It is here that a great jousting tournament occurred in 1434. A sign in Spanish marks the event, complete with a colorful picture of a knight and his steed both dressed in shining armor.

What I find even more fascinating are the huge storks nests built high on the church towers that we see as we walk into the village. And, just past Hospital de Orbigo, we reach "crowlandia," a grove of tall trees full of crows and their nests. A large scarecrow-like figure has been hoisted onto the top of a pole right in the middle of them in an effort, I guess, to keep those pesky crows away, apparently to no avail. Crows must recognize a fool when they see one. Better yet, maybe that foolish scarecrow, posted there to scare them away, has simply settled right in and become their friend—who knows.

We have a choice again and opt for the historic route toward Astorga. Old stone *bodegas*, or wine cellars, most likely still in use, are buried in the low grassy hills. We are now walking on a pleasant, flat, dirt path by a sea of bright yellow flowers. Blooming fruit trees add some shade to the mix. It is quite peaceful here and beautiful. I am reminded of why I enjoy the Camino so much as I think of nothing else but putting one foot in front of the other. Soon enough, we reach the Crucero de Santo Toribio, a large stone cross built on a circular tiered platform that overlooks the Camino and the valley below. Pilgrims have left their calling cards: small stones are piled up high at the foot of the cross. Astorga sits way off in the distance, its rooftops gleaming in the morning sun.

But before Astorga, the Camino has routed us into the small village of San Justo de la Vega. We have stopped here at a bar for coffee and a *tortilla Espanola*, a Spanish omelette, typical of the region, made with eggs and potatoes. Things get even more interesting now. Marcia reaches for her waist belt to pay, only to find it missing. I pay, and we rush out the door to find two pilgrims sitting at a table outside. One of them speaks both English and Spanish and calls back to Auberge Ana, last night's refugio, in San Martin del Camino. Ana exclaims excitedly they have the waist belt—but how to get back there? Our new friend hasn't skipped a beat, however, having also quickly called a local taxi for us. *Muchos gracias, Senor!* We are soon speeding backward on the main roads by the Camino on a wild Mad Hatter's ride to our destination. I say this with no exaggeration. Our esteemed taxi driver, not happy that we have asked him to slow down, speeds up even faster with unmistakable glee. I can't watch. I am slumped in the back seat of the cab with my eyes closed, holding on for dear life. He careens and screeches around curves and through villages until we finally reach the refugio. Marcia retrieves her waist belt, and we repeat the wild ride back to San Justo de la Vega. It must not be our time to die.

Shall I say, each step forward on the Camino is savored even more now as we are making our way toward Astorga—we have four more miles to go. The city is nestled beneath snow-peaked mountains which loom higher as we approach. I wonder, rather apprehensively, if the Camino will wind its way eventually through this mountain range too.

Getting into Astorga is an adventure all in itself. We pass first a life-size bronze statue of a modern pilgrim. He is gulping water from his trusty gourd held high in one hand while leaning on his walking stick with the other. Frankly, I haven't seen anybody drinking out of a gourd but him. Plastic water bottles are the order of the day. Yes, I know, I am thinking too much again. Next, we are tasked with crossing a canal. We walk a zigzag pattern back and forth via a huge elevated iron walkway and bridge to eventually reach the other side. I happen to look back and notice a simple road we missed that easily crosses the canal too. It is better not to look back sometimes—for obvious reasons. We must have taken the scenic route.

Astorga, which sits at the crossroads of the Camino Frances and the Ruta de la Plata (the Silver Route), is a large, bustling city full of tourists as well as pilgrims. We resist the urge to book beds at the municipal refugio we pass as we first enter the city. Of course, I insist we go check it out. Marcia is shaking her head by now and groaning, for she knows me well. "No, no, we'll find something else closer in. Come on—let's go." I agree, but it remains to be seen. The Camino takes us by the town hall in the main square of the city. Colorful flags are waving proudly in the warm breeze. People are milling around everywhere we look. My feet are starting to whine, and my back checked out an hour ago. Other refugios we pass are full, so we do what we always do on the Camino when we don't know what else to do—we walk on. Soon, we are on the other side of the city wondering what is left for us in the way of shelter for this night. The suspense lifts suddenly. A friendly Asian couple, who are fellow pilgrims, have shown up and steer us two blocks over (off the Camino) to the refugio where they are staying. We are relieved to reserve beds there too. Maybe we shouldn't be so surprised by our good fortune since we had both started our process of active faith and prayer in earnest just a few minutes before. I am awed just the same. What took us so long to pray and to ask?

Our refugio, interestingly enough, sits a short block or so from the fifteenth-century Catedral de Santa Maria de Astorga and the nineteenth-century Palacio Espiscopal, the Bishop's Palace. The Bishop's Palace was designed by the great, gaudy Spanish architect, Antonio Gaudi. We could not have booked a better location if we tried. And, we are out now refreshed and eager to see the sights. We start by walking the top of a portion of the old Roman wall that once surrounded and fortified the city. Next, we tour the museum associated with the Bishop's Palace. Astorga's history is rich and varied starting with its early settlement by the Celts, then the Romans, and later the Visigoths who were Germanic tribes. Legend has it also that both St. James and St. Paul preached in Astorga. The city was revitalized as

Walking West on the Camino—Encore Une Fois

pilgrims made their way west to Santiago de Compostela, and it became a major pilgrim halt. Astorga is also famous for its production of chocolate, the Mexican cacao bean having been brought over from the New World by Cortes.

We are quite fortunate to find the cathedral and its museum open. This Romanesque church, built in the eleventh century, was partially reconstructed later in the Gothic style. It is exquisite inside and out. Our Lady of Majesty, a statue of Mary and the Christ Child crafted in gold and silver, sits resplendent inside the nave. Also found here is another beautiful image of Mary dressed in sky-blue as well as one of St. James, the Peregrino. He is also depicted in a painting as the Moor slayer, riding his horse into battle. A dazzling collection of gold and silver chalices and jewels tops it all off like icing on a cake. The wealth and power of the Spanish monarchy, as well as that of the Church, stands in stark contrast to the Way of St. James and the pilgrimage. We grab an early supper and head back to our refugio and, yes, our bunk beds.

We are rested and anxious to head out early this morning. It is full steam ahead. Our walking guide warns us that we are entering the isolated region of the Maragateria and the high Montes de León. The Maragateria is a traditional area of stone houses with its own distinctive culture dating back to the Moors' presence here. But now, we are walking down flat, well-laid-out dirt roads amid scrub brush and then through several small villages, one being El Ganso. Its old stone church and bell tower form the centerpiece of this lovely little village. And, of course, we see storks roosting in a huge nest at the very top of the church tower, directly under an iron cross. Perhaps the birds find solace in the soulful toll of the bells, hour upon hour, just as the villagers surely do too.

We are noticing our path is beginning to climb through even scrubbier terrain. The white-peaked mountains stand just ahead. Purple patches of heather are everywhere. We also pass several gray horses grazing in the lush grass off the road. They look up curiously as we walk by. We have come almost eleven miles. We are hoping to reach Rabanal del Camino soon and to find beds there.

We are in luck. The British Confraternity of St. James, we discover, runs a beautiful old refugio off the narrow cobblestone street in the central part of this little picturesque village. It sits behind ancient stone walls just next door to a small Benedictine monastery. It feels like we have come home since the refugio is staffed by x-pilgrims, both men and women, from England. Soon enough, we are unpacked and out again, walking back down the narrow street to the local market to replenish our supplies (including cat food for some of the village cats). We return for their gracious afternoon teatime complete with an array of English teas and biscuits. A fire blazes in the large fireplace in the dining room, and pilgrims are gathered round it and around the table socializing, us included.

Later, we walk across the courtyard to the parish church of Santa Maria for their vespers and pilgrim blessing. One young monk is there officiating. Candles are glowing in the dim light. Once vespers ends, I unfortunately abandon all care in my excitement and rush up to the front of the church to take a picture of a beautiful image of Jesus on a simple cross. The monk, who is there to tend to the spiritual needs of the pilgrims, yells at me angrily, for I had not noticed that a small group of pilgrims had gathered at the side of the nave for individual blessings. I fight back hot tears of shame, apologize profusely, and leave quickly. His patience must wear thin sometimes dealing with so many of us. Nevertheless, I delete all the pictures of the monastery and church from my camera. I only wish I could delete the experience from my memory.

Still early this morning, we have walked into the almost abandoned village of Foncebadón. The remains of ancient stone houses sit in testament to bygone days. Other books on the Camino warn of a pack of wild dogs roaming this area—we find none. Even the dogs have moved on. After leaving the town and its heaps of rocks, we pass more lush pastures. Cows and horses are grazing by an old church, which is also in ruins. Soon after, we reach the Cruz de Ferro, a huge iron cross on a hill covered in more cairns. Peregrinos are congregating here for pictures. We join in.

We have been steadily climbing on the Camino. We read that now we will descend. And go down we most certainly do—on a long steep, rocky, treacherous path. There is no relief in sight. I pick my way slowly and carefully, my hiking poles steadying my climb down. I am not interested in another sprained ankle. And, did I fail to mention that it is a swelteringly hot day? We hear from other pilgrims that a hiker had to be carried out this morning. No surprise. White-peaked Monte Teleno, the highest mountain in the area, sits among the clouds in the distance. I can barely look up, I am so intent on looking down.

We are approaching the little village of El Acebo, with its distinctive slate roofs, nestled in the valley below. But first, we come upon a funky little ramshackle tourist shack an enterprising man has set up just for the discerning peregrino shopper. Flags of all nationalities hang from the ceiling. Camino shells and gourds crowd the counter. The man sits there grinning like the Cheshire cat. We buy some water for the cause and hurry on to the quiet little village of El Acebo.

After El Acebo, we have our sights on the village of Molinaseca five miles ahead. We will have walked almost sixteen miles today. We are still walking in high altitude, but our path takes us steadily down until we reach the rushing Río Meruelo and cross the Roman Puente de los Peregrinos (the Pilgrim's

Bridge) to enter the town. Just before the bridge, a young man is out in the late afternoon sun with flyers hawking his family's hostal. We make a mental note and walk on. Quaint restaurants line the river and offer tables, under bright umbrellas, by its banks. Were it not for the mosquitoes buzzing around us so incessantly, we might avail ourselves of a rest at one of them. Call it all good—timing is again key here.

It seems that Molinaseca is a haven for tourists and pilgrims alike, with its shops and restaurants and bars—its beautiful church towering over it all. The town has awakened from its afternoon nap. People are out en masse in the cobblestoned streets. We are tipped off again as to where to find lodging and head left until we reach Casa Rural San Nicolas. It is just down the street from the Iglesia de San Nicolas de Bari, the village's beautiful church (closed for now). Had we arrived at the hostal a few minutes later, we would have lost out. But we are able to book the last room complete with two little beds and an adjoining bathroom. Casa Rural is owned and run by a Brazilian family who are former pilgrims. We soon learn that it is the son and daughter-in-law's anniversary today, so they are not preparing their customary Brazilian cuisine for the pilgrims. They are heading out on a celebratory night of their own. Nevertheless, our kind host and his wife (the parents of that young man we encountered at the bridge) set about serving us huge slices of their homemade pound cake and making sure that we are comfortable. Now, it is my time for a siesta. I have dropped my backpack on the floor by my bed and, having rummaged around in the pack until I can rummage no more, I am soon fast asleep under real sheets and a lacy bedspread. My shower will have to wait.

By early evening, we walk back through the village and have dinner at the El Palacio Hostal Restaurante by the bridge—a cozy spot offering a good pilgrim menu. For nine euros, we have ordered up a lovely salad as a starter, cod and fries, bread and Spanish olive oil, ice cream for dessert, and, of course, vino tinto. On our way back to the hostal, we pass a fountain in the village square. A statue of St. James stands in the middle. It is another reminder that this lovely village was once a refuge for early pilgrims on the Camino and that it remains true to its calling to this very day.

Upon leaving Molinaseca, we soon catch a glimpse of misty Ponferrada sitting far off in the distance on the horizon. Ponferrada is a large city, and it takes us quite a while to reach the long iron bridge to enter the town. We detour off the Camino slightly to find an ATM in the commercial district and then retrace our steps and carry on into the old section of the city and by the thirteenth-century Knights Templar castle. Its exterior is fascinating indeed, with its old stone ramparts and towers. At the next village of Columbrianos, we stop for a rest at their church. More storks stand as sentinels in their huge nests high atop the church's bell tower. We walk on through the village of Fuentesnuevas and stop again in the church there. This church, with its lovely, round, painted ceiling, portrays Jesus and the apostles at the last supper. It also has a colorful retablo of St. James, the Peregrino. Our walk is mostly on flat surfaces today and through a string of small villages. In Camponaraya, we stop for a picnic lunch and, to our surprise, we meet up with a young woman from Arizona. She is traveling the Camino solo. We stop again in the next village of Cacabelos at the fifteenth-century Capilla de San Roque. St. Roch, who is so prominent in France but not so much in Spain, is another welcome surprise here. He sits majestically in front of a huge golden scallop shell, his dog at his feet, his robes raised characteristically showing the wound on his leg that never heals.

By the time we reach the large village of Villafranca del Bierzo, we have walked almost nineteen miles, most of it flat until the last few miles into the village. It felt like twenty-five miles. Yes, it was just a little stroll for a total of eleven hours. When we enter the city, we are two little exhausted drenched rats, sloshing through cold drizzling rain. Although this city was a major pilgrim halt, we have come too late in the day to see it. And, the refugios we pass are all booked full. Fortunately, we are kindly guided to seek out rooms at the El Cruce Hostal on the other side of the city, where we are able to secure a room. We have an early supper of fried calamari at the bar and then call it a day. In fact, I call it a good day, well spent. I only wish that we had dredged up the energy to walk over to the Iglesia de Santiago to see its famed doorway, the Puerta del Perdón (the Door of Pardon). There, in medieval times, the weak and the sick and the lame could enter and receive the same blessings and dispensations as those who completed the full journey to Santiago. But then, I think how many times in my own life I too must have walked through that door of pardon unawares.

Our walking guide gives us three choices leaving Villafranca. We choose the lower, less picturesque, but shorter route just off the road. The rain hasn't bothered to stop. We walk through a long tunnel under the mountains and then on the sidewalk. The road is on one side and the Río Burbia on the other. The sky is finally starting to clear as we carry on through several tiny villages and then reach Ruitelán and its refugio. We have come almost eleven miles. Marcia had read about the Albergue Pequeño Potala on the internet, especially that it offers a peaceful refuge and an excellent pilgrim meal. Soon enough, we are in a line to check in, in front of three friendly women from Italy. One speaks some English. It seems the two *hospitleros* are gone for the weekend, but they have left their refugio in good hands with a local man and his wife who are busily taking our euros and showing us our rooms. We have bunk beds in the same room as the three Italian women. By early evening, two Australians show up to claim the last two beds in our room—and the last two beds in the refugio, I might add.

Just before daylight, we are awakened by a lovely zen-like melody that wafts through the refugio reminding us that soon we must head out as they prepare for the next round of pilgrims. Our breakfast of mini cakes and bread and jam along with café con leche has been laid out on the long table in the great room. Excitement around the table prevails as we are all preparing to go on.

The grass is lush and green on the low hills and mountains as we walk by a rushing stream into the next little village of Herrerías. We manage to unload the rest of our cat food here, dumped on the porch of an abandoned shed where several cats and their kittens are curled up. They have found their own refugio of sorts. Horses graze nearby. Our walking guide recommends that we stay on the surfaced minor road and head straight for Laguna de Castilla from here if conditions are wet, thus bypassing the hamlet of La Faba. We see it perched on a steep ridgeline. Check! The sky is filled with rolling dark clouds. We are entering the rainy Galician region of northwest Spain now, heading up and up on the road into steeper mountains. I am energized, but Marcia is not. I guess my years living in higher altitude on the southern end of the Rocky Mountains, in New Mexico, has its advantages. We eventually reach the quaint little village of O Cebreiro (at 4, 264 feet).

O Cebreiro, a National Monument, is famous for its rounded, thatched-roof, stone dwellings built when the Celts occupied this region, some of these ancient homes still inhabited until recently. Crowds of people are milling around the entrance of the village having just been dropped off by tour buses. We are game to be tourists too and so explore one of the huts (called *pallozas*). I can only imagine what it must have been like to shelter here on dirt floors in the harsh winters. Fires must have kept them (as well as their livestock) snug and warm, as evidenced by smoke-blackened walls in the interior. We next weave in and out of a tourist shop or two and a crowded pub. We are no longer tempted by trinkets, having learned that lesson well on our past trips each year to the Camino. Or, is it just we didn't see anything we couldn't live without? Probably it is the latter—unfortunately.

We also visit the beautiful pre-Romanesque church of Santa Maria la Real (Royal St. Mary's) with its long rows of red votive candles all aglow. The soft candlelight illumines sacred relics found in a side chapel, one being a golden chalice said to be the Holy Grail from which Christ drank at the Last Supper. A statue of Mary and the Christ Child, called the 'Madonna of the Sacred Miracle", stands nearby. It is said that the statue turned her head in awe as the host and wine were turned into the blood and body of Christ one cold winter night sometime in the fourteenth century. It seems that a farmer had braved a blizzard to get there for the mass, much to the amazement of the local priest. The Eucharistic miracle is, to this day, associated with the legend of King Arthur and the Roundtable and the poem *Parsifal*.

Leaving O Cebreiro, we are walking up a road through pine trees and grassy clearings, where cows are grazing and ambling across our path. Poor Marcia is feeling the altitude and our continuing uphill climb in a way she can no longer ignore. She says she feels faint and exhausted. Fortunately, we have found a little store and restaurant in the next village of Liñares, and we sit for a rest and a snack for a long while and then cautiously plod on. What else can we do? We walk past a huge iron St. James, who is also shown plodding along, and then through the village of Hospital da Condesa until we get to Fonfría and its large refugio, the Albergue A Reboleira. It could not have come too soon. In fact, a nice young man has already escorted Marcia down the muddy road through chickens and roosters, her eyes closed. The cold rain has started up again. We also dodge the cows who are being herded through the streets to shelter for the night in their barns. Thank God we are able to book one double size bunk bed and pilgrim meals. Our new Aussi friends are here already, warming themselves by the fire. After claiming our bed (I volunteer for the inside by the wall) and dropping our packs, we rejoin them in a happy celebration. Just getting here without being plucked by helicopter off the mountain this day is cause enough to celebrate.

The albergue has a separate dining room in its own large palloza (grass-roof hut) just behind it. There we are served another wonderful communal-style pilgrim meal. We sit with our friends from Australia and others at the table and dine on a local bean soup, salade niçoise, their coarse bread and olive oil, huge platters of pasta bolognese, and, last but not least, the traditional Santiago almond tort. All this, including lodging and café con leche and toast for breakfast, totals twenty euros, or about twenty three dollars. After dinner, we hurry back through the rain, and soon enough, I am snuggled in next to Marcia, fast asleep. Our dormitory room is full of bunk beds packed with fellow pilgrims. We are fortunate to have found refuge here too.

I pull the hood of my jacket closer as we step out this morning, for the wind is brisk and cold. It is also barely light. We are headed for Samos today and the beautiful Samos Monastery, and we want to get there early. We have almost thirteen miles to walk this day. We descend among chestnut groves and oaks and then walk through several hamlets before we reach the village of Triacastela. There, we have a choice of two routes. But, of course, we are making a beeline for Samos and take the left path. We wind our way over several bridges crossing the Río Oribio and through more tiny hamlets. Villagers, along with a little brown cow-colored dog, are herding some of their cows down the Camino too. Up high on a stone wall, another dog and a goat are romping and playing together in the warmth of the sun. Father time stands almost still in this neck of the woods.

1998—Swinging the Botafumeiro at the Santiago Cathedral

The forest is beautiful in this area of rainy Galicia. It is a place where hobbits just might have staked out some of these huge, barrel-shaped trees alongside the path for their homes. The trees have spread their ivy-covered branches across the road, creating a leafy ceiling and another time tunnel through the woods. We walk on, and soon we are joined by our new Aussi friends who have come up from behind us. The glistening slate rooftops of the Monastery have come into majestic view. It is nestled in a dip in the hills in the valley of the Oribio. The sixth-century Benedictine Abbey of San Julian de Samos, another National Monument, once housed five-hundred monks; now, only a few remain. I read that the Asturias King Alfonso II was educated here. It was he who established the Cathedral in Compostela dedicated to Saint James. The Samos Monastery must have many more stories to tell—one small one being about that day eighteen years ago when I stepped off the curb at its gates, twisting my ankle badly and thus setting into motion my own journey on the Camino and my utter enthrallment with it. Despite that painful twist of fate, it is the sweetest *déjà vu* to be back here again.

Our Australian friends have booked ahead at a small hotel across from the monastery. I had hoped to stay at the monastery's refugio that is attached and sits just behind it, but Marcia vetoes that idea once we check it out. There is no heat, and rows and rows of bunk beds line the massive stone walls in a huge dormitory room. Old woolen blankets are stacked up. I find the refugio quite charming and well run, with its colorful painting high on one wall of St. James and his many pilgrims trudging along. We opt to stay where our friends are staying, but I make a mental note that I will be back someday, pulling one of those old blankets up to my nose, just as happy as can be.

After unpacking, Marcia and I are out slipping and sliding (but not falling) on the wet pavement in the rain, heading around the monastery for a tour of its church, its library, and its cloisters. A friendly monk is leading the tour. I am fascinated by a series of modern murals upstairs in the cloister that depict the monastic life of San Benito. In the mid-eighteenth century, San Benito joined the monastery at age fourteen and later became a brilliant writer and professor. One evocative mural depicts three monks huddled together in dark gray robes. Their faces covered by their hoods, they are sitting back to back in a circle reading large scholarly tomes. I am distracted by how cold it is in these monastery halls, and I imagine how great fires in the fireplaces and woolen robes must have kept the monks reasonably warm. I am wishing I had on one of those robes right about now. I am chilled to the bone. I see that Marcia's hands have turned a bright, chilly pink.

As it has started to clear, we walk over in the sunshine to the little ninth-century Mozarabic chapel of El Salvador, a reminder of Moorish influence from the past. We later catch dinner with our friends again and then return to our room for much needed sleep. Tonight, I am glad to be in our little private room.

The fog lies low in the valley as we head out this morning. It is barely light, but we have already had our coffee and toast at the bar. We want to carry on so as not to disturb the faster pace of our journey. We are heading for the large town of Sarria today and maybe beyond. We have been routed up a very muddy, narrow trail through the mountains as we climb up and out of the valley and then down again. Boo hoo—more *boue* or should I say *barr* (mud in Spanish). Our pilgrims' progress is slow and slippery and rather daunting until we leave the forest. By noon, we have come to Sarria, having walked through several little hamlets, including Hospital. In the Middle Ages, the hamlet of Hospital was apparently the site of a bustling pilgrim refugio also called a *hospital* (can we imagine why), hence its name.

Sarria was another pilgrim halt along the Camino in medieval times as it still is today. A word about Sarria—it is considered the final stretch on the Camino Frances, and it is also a popular starting point for many people who wish to walk only the last one hundred kilometers of the Camino and thereby earn the Compostela, the pilgrim's certificate or proof of the walk. We can't help but notice that the streets are crowded with pilgrims. There are those passing through like us, as well as those just starting out, congregating around tour buses and vans to begin their hike. We carry on. We have walked through the more modern part of Sarria and now climb several flights of stairs (the Escalinata Major) to reach the upper reaches of the town and its old section.

We stop for our picnic lunch here, and as we are resting and gazing out over the parts of Sarria from whence we came, up the long staircase come our Aussi friends. We are elated to see each other, but they are eager to find a restaurant for lunch. We bid adios and, soon enough, we are walking the old cobbled stone streets up to the top of the hill and out of the town. We have passed the remains of the castle of the counts of Lemos and its tower from bygone days as well as the old thirteenth-century Iglesia de San Salvador. We read that Sarria was also once the site of a medieval hospice and leprosarium, the Ermita de San Lazaro. Alfonso IX, the king of Leon, died in Sarria in 1230 on his own pilgrimage to Santiago. But now we must leave it. Our focus must be forward and not back. We press on.

Our path takes us down again on a gentle dirt footpath through the trees. We cross a medieval bridge, the Ponte Aspera, over the Río Celerio. We then cross another old mossy stepping stone bridge by a low-lying stream. These peaceful, lovely woods agree with me. The sun is out in full force now, and we are glad for the dappled shade among the tall oaks. We eventually reach the small village of Barbedelo and its refugio. Our Australian friends have booked here, but I say we go on since it is much too early to stop for the night yet. Or is it just bossy me? Marcia would have her way if she felt strongly that we should spend the night here, but she doesn't insist we stop.

By now, we are walking through another hamlet along the side of a small herd of cows who are ambling their way to their shelters for the night. Nearby, we come upon a *horreo*, a long, narrow corncrib on stone stilts common to this region in Galicia. As the afternoon sun starts to set, a cold drizzle returns, and we are anxious to find beds for the night. We find them in the village of Ferreiros at Casa Cruceiro. Yes, we manage to get the last two bunk beds. We have walked almost twenty miles this day. Can we stop now, Mommy dearest? We drag ourselves up to the dormitory room of bunks. We are oh so happy to have arrived—finally. We enjoy their very good pilgrim meal and then head off to bed.

It is cold again this morning and still rainy. We fortify ourselves with coffee and that delectable Spanish creation of eggs and potatoes and then head out. My feet are surprisingly holding up, and so are Marcia's. Passing through several more small villages, we can see the large town of Portomarín off in the distance. It is so near and yet so far. Just before the town, we come upon a large painted sign with explicit directions and a warning to take a detour straight into town. This diversion will bypass the road and traffic into Portomarín as well as a hairpin curve. That pretty little curvy paved road sits off to the left. Oh, had we only taken it. But no, we obediently follow the directions on the sign and soon enough find ourselves scrambling pitifully down scary large rock steps along a narrow, steep stone passageway to the street below. We can't go back, and we can barely go forward. It reminds me of a dream I had when I first started law school. I was this incredulous and puzzled bull standing on a long high slide, unable to get off as it carried me up and up. (I am a Taurus, the sign of the bull, so laugh now if you must.) By the time we reach the street, we are literally thanking God we didn't kill ourselves getting down that treacherous path. I suppose it was the safety of the local drivers, who most wanted to avoid us pilgrims coming into their town, that prompted that detour. Alrighty then. Here is my own safety warning, my dear fellow unsuspecting *peregrinos:* Take the hairpin curve—for God's sake!

We cross the street, walk down the road, turn left and walk across a very long modern bridge over the Río Mino and a reservoir. A little ruffled by now and distracted, we fail to read in our guidebook that we can bypass the town of Portomarin altogether and go left just past the bridge. Instead, we mount a long very steep flight of stairs into the town. This does afford us, however, an opportunity to replenish our supplies at a small mercado just up a cobbled street. The kindly old shopkeeper also points us back down the road where we can again get back on the Camino. Portomarín would have been a lovely place to visit, with its Romanesque church of San Nicholas, had we had more time. But carry on, we must. We pass by a factory or two in the outlying district and then by houses until we reach a rural area once again and then climb up into a more forested path.

I wish I could say that I have learned more patience by now, since this was, in fact, Saint James' early admonition—to be patient. Apparently, I am still learning that lesson. For, as it is starting to rain again, we are being passed by waves of hikers. One of them, this certain Frenchman, asks me in sketchy English (or was it French?) to reposition his rain cape atop his backpack. *Moi,* not understanding exactly what he wanted of me, did the best I could to oblige. He stomps off angrily, with a mutter, but not before I myself bark out my latest French expression that I had been practicing: "*Ne vous inquiétez pas.*" Don't worry! I should take my own advice. My anger startles me and most likely *le monsieur* as well as he dares not look back and continues up the trail and out of sight. It seems that we both must repeat *le première leçon* in patience. And just when I thought I was making some progress too. Or, is it that this incident brought me awareness, since only with awareness comes change. No excuses, you acted badly. *Pardon!*

We are determined to make a shorter day of it today. By mid-afternoon, we have walked through several more small villages and are now looking for beds for tonight. We eventually settle on staying at the only refugio (and restaurant) in the small village of Ventas de Narón. We have come twelve miles. We are fortunate indeed, for we are given bunk beds in one room among rows of other bunks but we end up being the only pilgrims in the room—our own private dormitory. It feels good to be here. I wonder if fellow pilgrims are just pressing onward in some race to make more time (and miles), extending their hectic lives to the Camino. Imagine that—*a rat race* on the Camino. But then, this is what we ourselves did yesterday, walking twenty miles. It is also true that there are days that ask twenty miles of us simply because we feel so good walking its rhythm.

Our pilgrim dinner is excellent: lightly fried fish, fries, a salad, Spanish bread and olive oil, ice cream for dessert, and vino tinto. The only rather annoying distraction is a table of peregrinos just outside the door to our room who are decidedly getting drunk and loud. Luckily, they are not bunking with us, and their commotion is past history as we both drift off very quickly into deep sleep.

Morning comes quickly again. This sweet family-run refugio is serving that most comforting ritual we never want to miss out on as we start our day so early: café con leche y tostada. After breakfast we leave the village, walking down the narrow paved road only to get hopelessly lost when the Camino leads off onto a dirt road among the trees. Puddles of standing water and mud from the recent rains must have drawn our attention down and not up to the next Camino yellow arrow. By the time we figure it out, it is too late to double back. We somehow get onto a paved road into the next village. We thankfully pick up the Camino again at yellow arrow signs that direct pilgrims off the road onto a dirt path through the woods—home sweet home. We could have headed off in the wrong direction, down some rabbit hole and through endless villages, but we didn't. By mid-morning, we have come to the hamlet of Portos and stop for awhile at "the spider bar" for an apple tart. Yes, decorative spiders climb the walls. As well, a huge metal sculpture of a spider sits in the side yard. It is all very odd, but maybe no different than those folks who collect frog things or teacups—oh well. *Muchas, muchas aranas!* We walk on.

We have walked through several villages, including Palas do Rei, Casanova, and then Leboreiro, with its beautiful little dark gray stone Romanesque church of Santa Maria. At times, rolling, puffy, white clouds are shielding the sun in the bright blue sky. We cross the stone bridge over the Río Seco heading now towards the large town of Melide. Between the villages today, we have walked forested paths that rival the beauty of any segment of the Camino. We are starting into the edge of green, lush eucalyptus woods. The strong fragrance of eucalyptus permeating the air is a healing balm to the senses. But by the time we have walked through Melide, it is starting to rain again, and the air has turned cold and damp. It is late into the afternoon, and we have come almost sixteen miles. Several of the hotels and refugios in town are full, but we have been told that there are two more on the other side of Melide. We locate one, the Albergue San Anton, where we are able to book two of the last bunk beds for the simple price of ten euros each—priceless to us. We have shed our dripping rain capes and claim our beds as the refugio quickly fills up. We have another early dinner at a bar just up the street and soon enough are back in our bunks for a cozy night's sleep.

The rain has ceased for a while, but the air is still humid and cool as we carry on out of Melide along a wooded path by more eucalyptus groves. Hoards of hikers are passing us by now, intent on making sure they get beds early, I guess. Marcia isn't taking any chances, however, and I suppose wisely books ahead on her smart phone at Albergue Touriste Ultrea in the relatively large town of Arzua almost nine miles away. It seems our focus now is on simply getting to Santiago and not just savoring the process—too bad. Reason rules the heart. Maybe it should this day.

We have walked through more hamlets and have crossed the old cobblestone bridge over the Río Iso into the pretty village of Ribadiso de Baixo with its distinctive red tile roofs glistening in the dewy mist. The sun is struggling to emerge from the clouds. Once at the refugio in Arzúa, we meet a woman who is walking the Camino Frances from St. Jean-Pied-de-Porte for the third time in three years—alone. She tells us that her husband, who misses her dreadfully, is crossly awaiting her return back home in Scotland. But she too must walk. She is seventy two years old. I read a blog not long ago of would-be pilgrims considering the pilgrimage at the age of sixty and whether they were too old to make the trip. Just go, I say. The Camino will toughen you up and take care of you and even revitalize you in the end. You will see.

By morning, the rains have returned, and Marcia, not to be outdone by our muchos fellow peregrinos, has booked ahead once more. She has found us a pension, or small private room, in the large town of Arca twelve more miles up the Camino. Fortunately so, for I am developing a nasty sore throat. The cold rain is taking its toll.

I am glad to have our own room. My nose is dripping like a faucet now, no matter what I take to try to make it better. Miserable and exhausted am I, and a bit disillusioned too, I might add. Could it be that the real world is encroaching, or is *this* the real world? As I drift off into sleep clutching my tissues and sopping my nose, I wonder.

This is our final day on the Camino before we reach Santiago de Compostela, almost thirteen miles away. It is truly bittersweet. Sleep has brought me some relief from my cold, but we must press on whether I feel like it or not. This morning, the cold drizzle is relentless. We finally come to the famous modern sculpture of Monte del Gozo known as "Mount Joy." Atop this hill, pilgrims get their first glimpse of the tall spires of the Cathedral at Santiago. Not so for us this day for, although it has stopped raining, the fog still lies low in the distance. Marcia decides we must follow a line of pilgrims across the hill and down a long, grassy, muddy trail. She is thinking that they are following a detour that will cut off some time and distance. But not so fast! We end up having to wander around for almost two miles until we catch a path through a deserted complex of buildings and then get back onto the Camino again. Beware the shortcuts or following those you believe know more than you do. My inner voice had told me to carry on the way we had been walking, but I had not listened to it—big lesson here.

We are only too happy to reach Santiago by early afternoon. But once here, it takes us quite a while to weave our way through the outlying commercial district before we reach the ancient section of the city. We are ever careful to follow the waymarks of the Camino. We are heading for the Albergue Seminario Menor, which we have read houses pilgrims. This stately, centuries-old facility sits high on a grassy hill overlooking Belvis Park, ten minutes from the cathedral. Once a Catholic seminary, it is now a refugio. We will be awed to join the ranks of pilgrims who have found refuge and rest here. We wind our way up the narrow cobbled streets, following the not-well-marked signs for the seminary, until we finally pass through its high stone walls at a gate. We then climb a long flight of stone stairs up to its vast entryway and registration room. The place is bustling with activity. It is mid-afternoon by now and time to find shelter. Our little beds are on the fourth floor, up more stairs. They are two in a sea of beds lining the long dormitory walls. Blankets are stacked high. We claim ours, for the night will bring a chill again.

Our backpacks sorted and stashed away, we are intent on finding the official Pilgrim Office where we will present our stamped pilgrim passports to claim our *Compostelas*. It is our proof of completion of the Way of Saint James, as though the proof of our journey is not already written into the Book of Life and deeply imprinted into the very fabric of our souls. We want our certificates just the same, enough so that we stand in a long line for over two hours, ever inching forward toward our prize. I suppose it is fitting and rather ironic that the Camino should end this way, this one final hurdle, and yes, a lesson in patience. Although there are many who will continue on to Finisterre on the Galician coast, we must take a train early tomorrow morning to Madrid, where we will catch our flight home the next day.

But first, we make our way over to the great Cathedral de Santiago for the evening mass. Only its outer front façade is covered in scaffolding for repairs, and the grand main entrance is blocked off. There is no longer any access for our eager fingers to touch the recesses at the Portico of Glory, where pilgrims have pressed their hands into the ancient pillar for eons of time. Those days are sadly gone. The thirteenth-century stone rendering of Jesus and the apostles at this entrance was the splendid work of Master Mateo. He placed a small statue of himself on one of the pillars here at the narthex, or entryway. We have no access to this either. I would have liked to bump my head against his, another tradition passed down through the centuries. Why? Apparently, it was done to receive some of his genius. I wanted to find out whether it worked.

The Cathedral is packed with people, parishioners and pilgrims alike. We crouch by one of its grand side pillars, and, as the mass concludes, I signal Marcia to follow me to the front of the nave, past the priests. We make our way behind the golden High Altar up the narrow staircase to a platform where a kindly old priest awaits. He welcomes us with a smile and hands us little cards depicting St. James with a blessing. Then, we do what others have done before us. We touch the massive, bejeweled and gilded image of the Great Apostle, give thanks for our buen Camino, and then climb quickly down the steps on the other side.

The remains and relics of Saint James are said to be buried here along with those of his two disciples—centuries ago removed from the graves resting under the sparkling, diamond-clad Milky Way near Padron. *Twinkle twinkle little star*. Now I know just what you are. At least I think I know. Now when I gaze at the starry night sky, my thoughts will return to the Camino and to the Way of St. James.

Below again, we see that the giant silver incense burner, the famous *Botafumeiro*, hangs motionless against a wall. Today, it is not for us to witness the spectacle of its swing in a vast arc just above the heads of the crowd, perfuming the nave with its smoky sweet fragrance, as I had experienced it many years before.

We stand out again on the Plaza del Obradoiro in front of the Cathedral and allow ourselves simply to be awed. To our right, on one full side of the grand plaza, sits the famous Hostal de los Reyes Catolicos (the Hostal of the Catholic Monarchs). Now a five star hotel and parador, it was once a pilgrim hospital. Its royal patrons were none other than Ferdinand and Isabella. It is said that the first ten pilgrims at its gate each morning receive free meals and lodging for up to three days. We do not try it. Maybe we will someday.

My mind flashes back to 1998. It is on this very plaza almost twenty years ago that I had hobbled around on my crutches—slumped over, sweaty, and exhausted. People were pointing and even snapping *my picture*. Now just imagine that. "A true pilgrim!" they exclaimed. If only they knew. If only I knew that my thirst for the Camino was yet unquenched and that I would return to walk it again and again, *encore une fois*.

I realize now that I had not really come here to heal my sprained ankle. I unwittingly had come to heal the broken places within me. I think back now, as I lay in bed in Samos those many years ago crying and asking God "Why me?" how truly gracious God was to allow this *twist of fate*. It set in motion a journey of a lifetime.

I also ponder what called me here? Saint James wrote that if we draw close to God, God will draw close to us (James 4:8). Perhaps it is here on the Camino, away from the rat race of my life, that I feel closest to the divine presence of God within. Yes, I walked the Camino, but really, the Camino walked me. It gently took my hand and led me ever forward. It showed me that I don't have to try to "figure things out" and that I can relax into the flow and the turn of the wheel of my life.

So just what did we learn on this pilgrimage of ours? I learned to step off the precipice and fly high—to let go and trust the process in life. Those leafy tunnels of time and even that snake Marcia almost stepped on taught us to live in the moment and not in the future or in the past. *Merci beaucoup, Mademoiselle Serpente!* Well done! Marcia learned all about courage as we crossed the path of those chickens and roosters and as we walked endlessly through those dense woods and high plateaus in the middle of nowhere.

We were reminded over and over that life is a mystery and that true wisdom comes in embracing it—in all of its aspects. Those red-and-white painted signs on trees and the brass shells imbedded in the sidewalks taught us that we are all interconnected in this great web of life we call the cosmos. I was instructed yet again that I am not alone here on planet earth and that unseen forces continually conspire to bring about my good. The synchronicities of our lives let us know this too, if only we are mindful enough to stop and notice. The Camino made us slow down, and watch, and listen, and wait.

Together, we learned to become strong and free, Marcia and I. Were we transformed by this sacred journey? Most decidedly so. Was our experience on the Camino all we wanted and hoped it would be? Yes, of course, and much more.

And, Saint James himself was ever present. He is that great archetype of trust and humility as the pilgrim and of strength and fierce courage as the moor slayer. We learned to walk more fully as both, on the Way and in our everyday lives in general.

As we are heading for the airport back in Madrid, I asked the Hilton driver just why he thought people come to walk the Camino. "It is good for the soul," he replied simply. It is the best answer I ever heard and the answer that rings most true for me. So, did my restless spirit beckon me here, or did the Camino itself call my soul? Back home again now in Santa Fe, the Way of Saint James whispers my name still. I suspect it always will.

Fini

Epilogue

After those last long days slogging our way down the muddy trails in the cold rain into Santiago de Compostela, Marcia and I most emphatically decided that this was our last trip on the Camino. *Fini!*

My, my how memories fade. We are now planning our next adventure on the Camino, starting this time in the ancient hilltop village of Vézelay, another UNESCO World Heritage Site, just south of Paris, in Burgundy. The Vézelay Route is one of the four major pilgrimage routes across France leading west to Santiago. The relics of Mary Magdelene are said to be housed there at the Basilique Ste. Marie-Magdeleine.

Come walk with us again. Or should I say *leap?* Ride the wind along with us beneath the dark starry sky. For now we know that the net will surely appear.

Pas fini

www.ingramcontent.com/pod-product-compliance
Lightning Source LLC
Chambersburg PA
CBHW040333300426
44113CB00021B/2742